Cierra Thurman

My Life:

The One He Never Got To Witness

For God,
who was always there,
even during my most challenging times.

Momma
you were the first example
of what a strong woman signifies.
I will forever cherish our bond
and closeness.

Brother,
although we grew up in a fatherless home,
I am so proud of the man you have become
and I know you will be
a great dad to your little baby girl.

Our family of three might be small,
and we don't always see eye to eye,
but we love each other unconditionally.

I Love You!

Cierra Thurman

My Life

The One He Never Got To Witness

Written Ambition Publishing

Cierra Thurman is a native from Chicago, Illinois. She was raised in a gang infested neighborhood where high crime rates and drugs were the norm. Cierra eventually moved to South Holland suburbs when her mother was financially able. She graduated from Thornwood High School in 2005. She received her bachelor's degree in Journalism and a minor in Criminal Justice in 2009 from Loyola University Chicago. Cierra played Division One basketball while attending Loyola, in addition to modeling. She worked at Cook County Jail as a deputy sheriff assigned to corrections before going back to Loyola, where she received her Master of Arts degree in Criminal Justice and Criminology in 2013. Currently Cierra was promoted to police officer with the Cook County Sheriff Police Department. In addition to her professional career in law enforcement, she is now a published author of her first book and much sought after motivational speaker. Her message is particularly geared to young women who may not have come from the best circumstances but are determined to not let their past dictate their future. When she is not traveling, Cierra enjoys working out, writing and cooking.

Table of Content

My Life:
The
One He
Never
Got To
Witness

Our Fathers

*I*t was a typical Wednesday evening for my mother and me as we walked into Valley Kingdom for her bible study class. Tonight the Pastor, Apostle H. Daniel Wilson, was teaching from the book of Matthew. He opened the class with a skit entitled "Our Fathers", which centered around four women and their relationships with their natural fathers.

The first woman's father was absent; he left her when she was five. All she recalls is her mother crying and her dad slamming the door behind him. The second woman was sexually molested by her father at the tender age of twelve. He touched her in places he shouldn't have, gave her candy and told her not to tell anyone. She told her mom anyway, but she refused to believe her. Even today, her relationships with men have continued to fail due to her lack of trust. The third woman never knew her father. She grew up knowing that he viewed her as a mistake and he left her mom once she refused to have an abortion. If she passed him on the street, she wouldn't know he was her father. The fourth and final woman had a great relationship with her father. He married her mom and took care of all the bills. She recalls spending plenty of time with him; she was his "little angel."

The bible study skit got me thinking about my own father. There I was, 22-years-old and reminiscing about a man I've never really known. Everyone talks about how stylish he was, how he dressed in collared shirts, slacks and dress shoes most of the time, and how he wore his hair in a Jeri curled afro, kept manicured nails and was quite charming. According to his sister, Jeanette, "He was a good looking brother with style and grace." Through family members, friends and photos, I've been able to educate myself about my father to some degree, but I still felt like I didn't really know the man he was.

Life doesn't treat everyone equally and we have to play the cards we're dealt. Whether you have an absentee parent, or have lost a parent, you'll be affected both emotionally and physically. Think about the relationship you have or have had with your own father and know that, whatever the circumstances may be, they're part of what made you who you are today. If you don't like the person you see in the mirror, now is the time to change your mindset and change your life. Spend ever increasing amounts of time becoming what you want to be and seeking the experiences you want to have. What doesn't kill you will inevitably make you stronger.

You'll just end up pregnant like your sister

Rose Brooks, my mom was raised in Haynes, Arkansas with her four sisters and five brothers. She was the youngest of ten and definitely regretted being the baby of the family. My Grandmother, Naomi, was highly overprotective and punished my mom for the mistakes that her sisters made. She forbade her from going to the school dances, screened her phone calls, and monitored her every move. Grandma was worse than the CIA. She didn't allow my mother to date until she was a senior in high school. Little did she know, my mom was listed in Lee Senior High School's year book as the "Biggest Flirt". My aunts all had boyfriends at an earlier age, but my grandma believed that they were "too fast for their own good" When my mom finally was allowed to have male company, it was always supervised. My granny would sit between them on the couch and watch her soap operas. She even tried to prevent Mom from going to college in spite of her full academic scholarship. "You'll just end up pregnant like your sister," shouted my grandmother.

My momma's sister, Deborah, got knocked up at Henderson State University in her freshman year, but Mom wasn't going to let Granny's fears and insinuations stop her so she rebelled, filled out the paperwork on her own and set off for the University of Arkansas at Pine Bluff. After graduating college in 1985, she came to Chicago with the intention of going to law school; however her plans were altered when she met my father.

> *Our parents almost always want what's best for us, and a loving parent never stops loving us, but they don't always see what's inside our heart. They may have a vision of our future and it may not correspond with what we see for our own future. If you feel passionately about something, write it down*

and show it to your parents. Seeing something in writing makes it more real, as does the act of writing it. It also helps to keep you from becoming overly emotional when you're trying to explain to them what it is you dream of doing with your life.

If you want something badly enough, don't let anyone stifle your goals and aspirations. Listen respectfully to their point of view. If you can't do what you want now, keep your dream close to your heart. Read, learn and set goals. When you're old enough, you can make your own choices. This is your dream and your life. When you follow it with passion and maturity, your parents won't feel as though you've abandoned them. If you follow your heart, they'll be proud of you.

Smooth operator

My mother got a job making programs at Taylor's Funeral Home on the South side of Chicago. One day while waiting on the bus stop at 79th and King Drive after work, she was approached by a peddler asking for money. When she turned him down, he got aggressive, and that's when the man who would become my father, Billy, came to the rescue.

"Hey, Sweet Thang, can you spare a dollar?"

"Sorry, no."

"What's the matter? You think you too good or something? You look like you can afford it!"

At this point, Billy stood in front of the man and said, "Nigga, you better stop bothering my woman. Now move along."

My mother was relieved and really flattered. She thanked Billy for his kindness and he jokingly made fun of the way she talked. He knew immediately that she was from the South.

"Where you from girl?" he asked.

"Haynes, Arkansas," admitted my mother with her southern accent. When the bus came, my dad rode with her until she got to her stop at 41st and King Drive where she stayed with her aunt, Lena. The next day when my mother approached the bus stop at 79th, there was my father waiting for her. He repeated the same ride from the previous day and when my mother reached her stop this time, he asked her for her phone number. She really liked him so naturally she played hard to get and turned him down gently.

"You seem like a nice enough man, I just don't know nuthin' 'bout you," she grinned. "Sorry, Mister, I can't give you my number."

From what I've been told, my father was accustomed to getting everything he wanted, so he was persistent in pursuing her. Finally, after a week of bus rides they exchanged numbers. My father was a smooth operator and swept my mom off her feet. He told her everything that a woman wanted to hear. My mom lacked the experience of dealing with men because of her sheltered childhood, so she fell for everything that came out of his mouth. A month into their relationship, she discovered that she was pregnant, so she moved in with my dad on 78th and South Shore Drive. At the beginning of the relationship, Billy told her that he was a real estate agent, but it didn't take long for my mother to figure out that he was not in the house selling business.

You may have heard the expression "actions speak louder than words". This is particularly true in relationships. People can say anything because words are free, but when they back it up with actions, we are more likely to trust and believe them. A man who loves a woman will show his love in countless ways. They don't need to be big or expensive gestures.

In a world where texts, tweets, and email have virtually eliminated the need for communication through human interaction, it's become easy to manufacture words that are meaningless. On the other hand, if you've had some bad experiences with men, don't assume one way or the other with your next man. Don't bring the sins of the past and lay them onto a new relationship.

Take what he says and let it sit for a while. Don't just believe what he says, believe what he shows you. And after he shows you, believe him.

Never get high off your own supply

illy lied so much that it seemed as if he actually started believing the lies coming out his mouth. My mom caught him up so many times that finally one day he confessed to being a drug dealer. When my mother shared the news with her supervisor/best friend, Ester, she insisted that my mother end the relationship.

"Rose, messing around with a hustler is a bad idea. You a good woman, you don't want to get into no trouble."

After several warnings from Ester, my mother became almost certain that her boyfriend was hiding more secrets. She questioned him about other women and asked if he had any children. For a while he continued on with his dishonesty, but my mom was unwavering and he finally confessed to having a daughter named Shaunta.

"So are you still involved with yo' baby's mama?" she asked.

My father assured her, "I don't get along with my baby mama. Shit, only time I see her is when I visit my daughter."

My father must have seen my mother's insecurities building. She told me that he got down on one knee and proposed right then and there. He insisted that they travel back to Arkansas to get married. That way all of her family members could witness this special occasion, and he continued on with his smooth techniques once he met my mother's family. Not only was he a good looking man, but he was also the perfect gentleman; opening doors and kissing hands, too.

Up to that point, the trip down South was a success. The only thing left to do was walk down the aisle. Too bad my father had to get drunk before he said his "I Do." And instead of a romantic honeymoon, my dad continued to drink with my Uncle Larry, so my mom basically spent her wedding night alone.

My mom had thought he was such a gentleman but when

they got back to Chicago he began to reveal his true colors. First, he stopped picking her up from work, even though my mom had bought the car; he was cruising around in her ride. By this time she was six months pregnant with me, and she was so pissed off because she had a brand new car and was still stuck riding the damn bus home.

One day, she was surprised to come home to an apartment full of strangers. But she was even more shocked to witness my dad snorting cocaine. He was supposed to be selling the drugs, not using them. He had broken the number one rule of a drug dealer; never get high off your own supply. My mother went off and my father pushed her into the bedroom where they would finish their argument.

When he got tired of explaining himself, he slapped her in the face and shouted, "Stay the fuck in the bedroom!" This was the first time my father hit my mother, but it would not be the last.

You don't always get what you want. That doesn't mean you should just settle for less than you deserve. It's never OK for a man to hit a woman (and vice versa). No one deserves to be mistreated either physically, verbally or emotionally.

Too often, we get a gut instinct about something or someone and we casually justify not paying attention to that. Learn to trust your instincts and intuition because your gut will never steer you wrong.

Mr. Nice Guy

He assured my mom that his drug usage was under control but my mom didn't believe him.

"He drank too much and smoked too much. I knew the drugs were changing him. I could tell by his eyes." Here she describes the worse beating she ever received from my father.

He came home one day really pissed off. "Bitch, you on that shit again, huh." She wasn't prepared when he punched her dead in her face and didn't stop until he grew restless. He hollered that my mom was cheating on him because he found a man's wallet in their car. My mother was confused, bruised, and bloody and screamed that she didn't know who the wallet belonged to. Twenty minutes later his best friend, Mike, knocked at the door. He came to retrieve his wallet, which he accidently left in the car. My mom overheard their conversation and came out of the room.

Mike seemed concern when he asked, "What happened to you?"

My mom replied, "I got my ass beat because you left your wallet in our car."

That's when reality set in; my mom was married to an abusive drug user. The next day at work, Ester saw the bruises. My mother lied to cover up for my father, but Ester knew better and warned my mom once again to leave him. But my mother was scared to leave my dad; she was almost eight months pregnant and hoped that my birth would make the situation better. My mom suffered intense pregnancy craving when she was expecting me. Her particular food of choice was fried shrimp. My dad would bring her some almost every day, often without her even asking for it. She jokes that my birthmark resembles a shrimp because she ate it so much while she was pregnant.

He took her out to lounges where he taught her how to dance and shoot pool. Despite my father's efforts (to this day she still ain't got no rhythm), he never could quite teach her what came natural for him. When he danced, all eyes were on him. He had this presence about himself that drew people in. Whenever they made up after an argument, they celebrated with a night out on the town.

"He loved for us to dress alike," she revealed. "Everything wasn't always bad." My mom was convinced that my father would change his ways. Sadly, it became a regular routine to come home to a house full of people smoking crack cocaine.

Soon my dad began taking her checks from her, leaving her without any money at all. One day my mom refused to give up her check. That was a very bad decision on her part. My father was extremely drunk and beat her severely. He slapped her around and even kicked her in the stomach. She was frightened for her unborn child (that would be me) so she went to her Aunt Lena's home. Instead of calling the police or allowing my mother to stay, Aunt Lena encouraged my mom to go back home.

"You are his wife and you all need to work this out." With no other place to turn, my mom went back home to my apologetic father who promised that he would never hit her again. He bought her gifts and for a brief moment in time things were back to the way they were when they first met. But as you probably have already figured out, it didn't stay that way for long.

My mother got a little smarter and stopped telling my father how much she was making. Her friend, Ester, showed her how to cash her checks at the Currency Exchange so that she would have some money in her pocket. She was forced to pay the bills because my father was becoming less of a drug dealer and more of a coke head as he continued using his own product. She was not making enough money at the funeral home. With her Bachelor's Degree in Criminal Justice and a friend in the department, she had little difficulty landing a position as a clerk in the Cook County Law Library.

My mommy was getting closer and closer to her delivery date so she got my father's sister, Aunt Bunny, to spend nights with her to prevent my father from jumping on her. They became really good friends and she admitted everything that my dad had been doing. My father was "Mr. Nice Guy" whenever other people came around. He was very charming and loving in the presence of his family and friends, and would go out of his way putting on the "good guy" act to cover up for what went on behind closed doors. My mother, on the other hand, wore concealer and over-sized black sunglasses to shield her bruises and her pain.

Domestic violence is a difficult topic to discuss, and because of this, many cases of domestic violence go unreported. Both men and woman can be abusers and it remains behind closed doors where the abusers continue to create excuses for their behavior and continue to abuse.

They may promise that it will never happen again, blame it on their temper, the drinking or drugs, or their friends' influence. They'll say they're sorry and they'll continue to abuse. They often threaten further hurt if you report them or say anything or try to leave. If there are children involved, it makes things more complicated and even more dangerous.

Heed the warning signs early. Find a domestic violence center or contact your local police department for help and guidance to centers near you. Don't keep domestic violence locked up. Find out how you can get yourself (and your children) to safety as soon as possible.

Daddy's little girl

All during Mom's pregnancy, my dad denied that I was his. However, when I was born he instantly fell in love with me because I came out looking just like him. They named me Cierra Tasharae Thurman after the Sierra Mountains (apparently they weren't sure about the spelling), and my middle name, which supposedly means something profound in the African culture, came from some baby book.

I was birthed February 19, 1987 at Mercy Hospital in Chicago, Illinois weighing in at 8 lbs and 6 oz. It took my mother 16 hours to introduce me to the world, but I came out healthy with sandy brown hair and slanted dark brown eyes. After I was born, my dad stopped having his doubts and believe it or not, he even stopped hitting my mother. He was a great father and was working towards becoming a better husband. My mother told me he used to hold me in his arms for hours at a time and constantly play with me.

"I had to make him put you down so I could change your diapers," smiled Mom, as she told me the story.

I like when she talks about him because I don't have one single memory of my father from my childhood. All I know is that growing up I didn't have one. As an adult, I find myself mourning the loss of all the memories I never got to share with him. I find myself missing the relationship with my father that I never had the chance to develop.

Sometimes my mom and I browse through old photo albums and she tells me what he was like. He used to remind her to call and check on her parents down south. Even if she wouldn't admit it, he knew she was home sick. He stood 6'3" and she told me he played pickup basketball games at the park on the weekend with his friends. The one thing that sticks out in my mom's mind the most about my father is how much he liked taking photos.

"Everywhere we went it was like a photo shoot. He thought he was a pretty boy," she grinned.

I play basketball, I model, and I defiantly got my dance skills from my old man, I thought.

It's amazing how much we have in common. Even though I did not know him personally, somehow I've come to know him so well. When I least expect it, I'm reminded of the missing piece in my life.

I used to envy my friends when they talked about the things that they did with their fathers. I wanted to be Daddy's Little Girl, but unfortunately that was not possible because no matter how often I prayed to the man above, and believe me, I prayed every night, he just didn't want to bring my daddy back.

Life may not always be fair, but one think I've come to learn is that envy is a waste of time and energy. You probably have everything you need and the sooner you realize that, the more you'll come to appreciate your life and the people around you. Remember, God has a plan for your life and it's your job to focus your energy on edifying others and working toward your heart's desire, provided it's within His Will. We're given certain trials for a reason. For me, perhaps having my dad taken from me is what gave me the heart to love and to be the woman I am today.

Rose, Billy is gone

After my mom had me, she didn't waste any time before she was knocked up again. She wanted to have an abortion because she didn't think that they could afford another child, but my father insisted that she have the baby.

"This could be my little boy," he told her. So my mother went through another pregnancy. Turns out, my daddy was right.

On July 7th, 1988 she gave birth to my beautiful baby brother, Courtney.

My dad held my brother proudly in his arms, and then announced that he would rush home to get my mom a change of clothes. Six hours later, he had not returned. Instead my dad's sister arrived with a Catholic priest, though my mom was a Baptist.

I was barely walking when my father was killed.

"Rose, Billy is gone," said Aunt Madie. My mom was confused, where could her husband possibly be when he was supposed to be picking her up from the hospital? My Aunt Madie tried to explain again, this time with more clarity.

"Rose, Billy was killed this morning by the Chicago Police."

My mother couldn't believe what she was hearing. The father of her two children was no longer living. She immediately went into a state of denial and refused to accept what her sister-in-law was telling her. The officers would not give any family members information about the death of my father. They would only speak to the wife of the deceased so she was escorted down to the police station.

There she discovered that my father was celebrating the birth of his first son and snorting cocaine with his cousin, Leroy. He got a little paranoid and swore that someone was trying to break into the apartment. He was so high that he called the police himself. Leroy tried to calm him down, but since the call had already been made, he immediately started cleaning up and flushing the drugs down the toilet. When the police arrived at the front door, my dad thought that it was the burglars and continued to behave irrationally.

The police proceeded to kick the door down, and after evaluating the scene, they let Leroy out as they attempted to calm my father down. What happened after Leroy left is unclear, but whatever happened, it resulted in my father being shot five times in his back.

My mother went to the morgue to identify the body and hardly recognized him. His face was severely darkened. She was told by the examiner that the bullets had hit vital organs and drained all the blood from his body. Seeing him lying on the table confirmed what everyone had been saying; her husband was DEAD.

> *One of the most profound things about death is that it can't actually teach us about life. We go through life worrying about things that help us survive, but we forget that God provides us with all we need. We*

pay our bills, compete for the best jobs or positions, and strive for more and better "stuff", all the while losing our focus for what's really important - the people we love, our friends, family and relationships.

Live life and make memories. Create experiences for yourself and think of the well-being of others. Ask yourself "What would it take to make me happy?" When you find the deepest inclination of your heart, go after it without hurting those who might get in your way. And on your life's path, LIVE!

Old country Bamma

My earliest memory as a child was attending my father's funeral. Everyone was dressed in all black and my mom cried a lot, but at the time I didn't understand why. My mother's side of the family traveled from Arkansas to pay their final respects and comfort my grieving mother. The repast was held at Grandma Mary's home on 82nd and Eberhart. The apartment was crowded with people mourning my dad's death. Overwhelming aromas filled the air of the different foods brought in. Grandma Naomi tried to convince my mom to move back to the South.

"Baby girl this ain't no place to raise 'dem children. You all by yo' lonesome in this big 'ole city. Come home with yo' folks." Despite her situation, my mother did not want to move back home, she had outgrown the country life.

"Mom, I'm okay." My Grandma left the conversation alone for the moment but was determined to get her youngest daughter back to Arkansas. Later that day both my grandmothers got into a heated argument. Grandma Naomi accused Grandma Mary of stealing from my mother.

"I saw you Mary, you was stealing from my baby girl. You took some money out of 'dem envelopes 'dem people been leaving her."

Mary quickly shouted back, "Look hear you old country bamma, I don't have any reason to steal anything."

Grandma Naomi screamed, "I saw you! You ain't nothin' but a low down dirty thief, come on baby girl we outta here." And just like that, my family members quickly assembled and we left Grandma Mary's home. My Grandma Naomi had seen enough.

"Robin, you comin' home with me. You don't belong here and you need help with dos kids." My mother pleaded and pleaded with my grandma, trying to convince her that our family of three would be okay.

Her last words to my grandma were, "Ma, God knows how much we can bear."

My grandmother was a God fearing woman and had raised her kids in church, so with that she was confident that her daughter could make it. My mama wasn't alone after all because she had God by her side. The next day my maternal family left and went back to Arkansas, and we moved in with Grandma Mary.

> *No matter what trials and tribulations you face in your life, remember that you can always go home. Home is a safe and secure place where you will have the support and comfort of your family. Recognize the blessing this is and don't let pride or shame keep you from taking refuge with your loved ones.*

That's my husband you talking about

My mother sued the City of Chicago for the wrongful death of my father. The city was willingly to settle out of court for 1.2 million dollars, but before the judge awarded my mother with the money, another woman marched into the courtroom and said, "That's my husband you talking about."

My mother stood there in disbelief, holding her marriage certificate. Unfortunately, the mysterious woman had her marriage certificate too, but with an earlier date. My mom nearly fainted once she realized that the lady was telling the truth. Tears rolled down her face as she became conscious of the fact that she had married a bigamist.

My father was separated from his first wife, but they never legally divorced. And just like that, with the proper evidence, the courts rewarded the money from the lawsuit to Brenda, his first wife. Brenda walked out the courtroom that day with 1.2 million dollars.

Despite winning all the money from the lawsuit, she did not get the opportunity to spend it. It turned out she had different aliases with several distinct social security numbers. She was placed in jail after the judge discovered that she was collecting money illegally through the welfare system. My brother, half-sister and I were each given five thousand dollars, but after the attorneys were paid, my mother reimbursed for the funds spent on my dad's funeral arrangements, and the City got back the money Brenda had been stealing, all of the cash was gone.

After the court had made its decision, my mother went back to my Grandma Mary's home and overheard my Uncle Pumpkin (dad's brother) arguing with her. He revealed that Grandma Mary knew about Brenda the entire time and she was the one who told her about the lawsuit and where the trial was being held.

"You've been cheating Rose out the rent money. You told her that it was $600 dollars a month." Grandma Mary snapped back.

"You need to mind your own damn business and stop worrying about what I'm doing under my roof."

"When I see her, I'm gone tell her the truth," warned Uncle Pumpkin. "You got Rose paying $300 and the rent ain't nothin' but $400."

When my grandma turned around, she saw my mom standing there and she knew that she had heard the whole conversation. My mom didn't have to say a thing to Grandma Mary because her eyes said it all. She had had enough and quickly packed up our things and moved in with my Uncle Pumpkin and his girlfriend, Toni. That living arrangement didn't last long because Toni became frustrated with another women living in her home, so once again we packed up and left. This was around the time my mother met and fell in love with a man named Johnny.

Johnny was a known hustler, but he was also extremely charming and very generous. After he found out about my mother's situation, he moved us into an apartment on

78th and Kingston. My mom knew that getting involved with another drug dealer was not a good decision but she needed help financially and Johnny provided her with that. I was about four years old then and my brother had just turned two. At the time, Johnny was the only father we had ever really known. He spent time with us, tucked us in bed at night, and spoiled us rotten. He bought us whatever we wanted, new toys, shoes, and clothes. My mom didn't approve of the way he got his money but she sure didn't have a problem with spending it. One day my younger brother and I were watching television in the living room when the cops showed up to the front door. They had a search warrant in my mother's name. They knew she was dating Johnny and since the apartment was in her name and Johnny was nowhere to be found, they arrested her instead.

As they cuffed my mother, I screamed for them to stop. My brother and I held tightly onto her legs and cried.

"Please don't take my Mommy away. Leave us alone! I remember my mother crying as well. She tried to hold back her tears and told one of the officers to call my Aunt Bunny to baby-sit us.

As my mother was escorted out of our home, my brother and I fought the policeman who tried to restrain us. And just like that my mother was gone! The next thing I remember was waking up at my aunt's house. I got out of bed and questioned her about my mother's whereabouts.

"Where did those men take my Mommy," I asked?

Instead of giving me a straight answer, she just sent me back to bed. "Cierra, your mom will be back soon, now get back in bed and make sure you do not wake your brother."

I got back into bed like I was told and put my arm around my little brother. At the time I wasn't sure if I would ever see our mom again. Meanwhile, my mother was locked up in the Cook County jail being interviewed by the very people that she worked with. I can only imagine her embarrassment. After three days, Johnny hired and attorney and got my mother out of jail, but three days can seem like an eternity when you're young and don't have the slightest idea about your parents whereabouts.

On the third day of our separation, my mother and Johnny burst into the room at Aunt Bunny's house and hugged and kissed us. I was so happy to see them again and, although my brother does not recall this scene from his childhood, I knew that he was just as ecstatic as I was. Our reunion was wonderful and I hoped that we would never have to part again.

For a while, things were good in our household. Everything seemed to be back to normal and for a short time I forgot all about our brief parting from our parents. I didn't remember until the exact same thing reoccurred, but this time the police were taking Johnny away from us, the only father figure in our lives. And this time he would be gone for more than three days. Johnny was sentenced to fourteen years in prison. When he left us, I was six years old and my brother, Courtney, was only four. My mother took us to visit Johnny and we wrote him letters, but she vowed to never get involved with a drug dealer again.

They say that insanity is repeating the same mistakes over and over and expecting a different outcome. If we step back from a situation and look for patterns, we'll often fin them, whether good or bad. Learn to recognize the things that are making your relationships miserable and stop repeating those patterns. If you're not sure about what to do, don't do anything until you are sure.

For me, I've considered seeing a qualified counselor to help me understand some of my beliefs about men and to find healthy ways to address those perceptions so I don't keep making the same mistakes.

Being both parents

When my brother got older, he began to question my mother about our father, Johnny. He didn't know that Johnny was not our real father. He didn't know that our mother was actually the chick on the side. He didn't know that Johnny lived with the mother of his own children; he only came to visit us. He didn't know how much Johnny's mother disliked our momma for being a home-wrecker. One day his mother, Madea, got fed up and told my mom off.

"You know he married right?"

"He ain't married. I know he got a girlfriend though."

"That's the same thing," Madea protested. "Little girl, you're destroying a family.

"You can't destroy what's already broken," my mother said rolling her eyes. My mom knew what she was doing. She kept a low profile and she understood her role. It wasn't her fault that his woman didn't satisfy his needs. Johnny was breaking bread and taking care of us so my mother was more than willing to take on the duties that his main chick couldn't handle.

One day my mom took Courtney by the hand, sat him down, and showed him pictures of his real dad. My brother asked questions and my mom answered them in a way she thought he would understand.

"Mommy where is my Daddy?"

"Courtney, your father is in heaven."

"I thought he was in jail."

"No son, your real father is in heaven, here are some pictures of him."

"Where's heaven?" Courtney wondered.

"It's the place that the preacher talks about in church; your father is looking down on you right now." My mom seemed to get emotional so she excused herself to go to her bedroom saying she had to make a phone call. I knew that she did not have to make a phone call. I knew because

I heard her crying. I tried to entertain my little brother, while my mom regained her composure.

"Our father was killed a long time ago, but luckily we have a mom who plays both of those roles," I whispered.

After our small talk, my brother went into our mother's room and said, "Mom, I'm glad that you can be our Mommy and Daddy." I could tell that my mom was no longer sad and my brother's words were more encouraging than he could have ever imagined.

Although I almost never cried in front of my mother and brother and seemed to have a positive outlook on our situation, I used to think it was unfair that Mom had to struggle to make ends meet. I knew it would be better if we had a man in the house to help out with things. My brother was always trying to get some new clothes or shoes. He had grown accustomed to Johnny's wealth. My mom always tried to be fair, but sometimes he would get new things and I wouldn't. I knew that she loved us equally, but I was still hurt when she spoiled him with a new pair of shoes and I was stuck with my old ones. My mom explained to me that I was far wiser than my years and right now Courtney did not fully understand.

Since that conversation with my mother, I took it upon myself to be self sufficient.

My mom use to say, "I ain't really worried about you. I know you can take care of yourself."

I was the independent child and my brother needed a little more guidance. She used to tell me that we have to play the hand we were dealt, so I stopped feeling sorry for myself. Besides if my mom could handle things, then I could, too.

I learned from an early age to "play the hand I was dealt". That means I always made the best of any situation. We can always find something bad about our circumstances or the people in our lives, and sometimes it's not as easy to find something good, but you'll be a much happier and healthier person if you can find a way to do this. It's all about knowing how to play the cards to your best advantage.

Successful people don't whine and complain because they have to work their way to the top. They don't use setbacks as an excuse to quit and they don't blame others for holding them back. The sooner you recognize that you're in charge of your own happiness, the sooner you'll reach a point where your happiness is unshakeable.

Babysitter from hell

Ever since I could remember, it was just the three of us: Me, my mom, and my little brother. My mother did have boyfriends and when I was little she told me they were my uncles. But one day I saw my mother kissing my uncle and even though I was young, I knew that they weren't supposed to be kissing each other in the mouth and using their tongues. When I asked her, she stopped saying the guys were my uncles.

I was about six when I really started missing my dad. Since I knew he wasn't ever coming back, I had to be strong. My mom was forced to work two jobs and since we could not afford babysitters, it wasn't long before I took on that role. Well actually, we couldn't afford a quality caregiver and each one we could afford turned out to be a Babysitter from Hell.

My most memorable babysitter was a friend of the family named Jeanette. My mom met her while we were staying at my Uncle Pumpkin's house. Jeanette was Uncle Pumpkin's baby mamma's aunt. Did you catch all that? A bit confusing, I know. She and my mom became good friends. She was funny, talked a lot of shit and made money anyway she could. "She was a go-getter," remembers my mom.

One day, my mom was called in unexpectedly to work her second job and Jeanette offered to babysit. "Girl, I'll watch them for you." My mom didn't hesitate before she scrabbled out the crib on her way to work leaving me and my brother behind with a 6 foot, 240 pound giant. Her attire consisted of a pair of blue jeans and a loose fitting T-shirt to minimize her large stomach. The only jewelry she owned was a pair of small gold hoop earrings. Her eyes were bigger than Tracey Ellis-Ross (you know the character, Joan, on the sitcom Girlfriends) and she brushed her hair back in a low ponytail. Her short stubby fingernails were even more noticeable while she puffed on a long Benson & Hedges cigarette.

The first night, Jeanette seemed like a decent babysitter; she prepared peanut butter and jelly sandwiches, played games and read us a bedtime story before putting us to sleep. That didn't last long because the next thing I remember is seeing her snooping around in my mother's room. I called my mom on her cell phone immediately to tell on Jeanette.

"Mom, Jeanette is up in the ceiling," I whispered.

"What?"

"Yeah, I see her standing on yo' bed lifting up yo' ceiling."

"All, hell naw, my money up there," exclaimed my mother. When my mom got home, she questioned Jeanette about the drop ceiling in our basement apartment. Jeanette looked at me out of the corner of her eyes and denied everything.

"That little girl ain't seen me do nothing. I don't know why you believe them kids. You know they be lying."

I wasn't the one being deceitful, Jeanette was. My mom knew it too, but she didn't get rid of her. She needed her. She had yet to establish a stable sitter and Jeanette was conveniently located around the corner. The next incident my mother recollects is when Jeanette and her sister, Peaches, came over to kick-it one night. It was a weekend and they didn't have anything to do, so Jeanette suggested that they get some liquor, smoke some weed and play some cards. It seemed like a good idea until Jeanette persuaded them to turn up the stakes on a friendly game and place a wager.

"Let's play for money," insisted Jeanette. Both Peaches and my mom knew why she wanted to all of sudden play Blackjack 21.

"Weed wasn't her thang, crack was" explained my mom. Long story short, Jeanette ended up loosing her money and tried to bully her younger sister to forking over her cash.

"Yeah, Bitch, gimme my money back. You was cheating."

My mother intervened. "She wasn't cheating, Jeanette."

"Aw fuck that, fuck that, I'm getting my money back. Motherfuckers ain't taking my shit."

Jeanette attempted to fight Peaches in the kitchen, but Peaches escaped her grasp and ran off with her money leaving my mom behind to fight her battle. Next, Jeanette turned her attention to my mother.

"You let her leave so I'm getting some of my money back from you."

My mama stood tall, even though she barely came to Jeanette's shoulder and emphasized "I ain't Peaches, I ain't scared of you. Now get the fuck out of my house."

You would think that by now, my mom would have learned her lesson and started looking for another babysitter, but no, that's just too much like right. She kept Jeanette on to babysit again, even after the card game had gone bad. When Jeanette finally did leave, it was of her own accord.

"Rose, I'm leaving," she ranted. "They gone be 'aight. They grown anyway. They keep on watching me, sheeeeeeeit, they should be able to watch there damn selves."

After Jeanette finally left, Versa came into our lives. She was a skinny light skinned woman who rocked a high top fade like Kid from the movie Kid n' Play. One of her legs was much shorter than the other so she would skip down the street with me and my brother to school. She would cook dinner and help us with our homework, even though math wasn't her best subject. Jeanette began to notice how permanent Versa had become and got jealous. She would say negative things about her on regular basis.

"You ain't nothing but a cripple dumb bitch." You see, Jeanette was from the streets so she talked shit to anybody, especially if she felt like she could intimidate them.

One day I overheard Versa crying on the phone talking to my mom, "She made me get high, I didn't want to do it, but she made me get high." She was referring to Jeanette who forced her to smoke crack cocaine.

She had put the pipe up to Versa's mouth and said, "Gone bitch, try this, this shit good for you."

Versa was scared of Jeanette so she took the pipe and smoked it. Once again my mom confronted Jeanette about her misbehavior but Jeanette just shrugged it off.

"That Bitch wanted to get high," she said. Jeanette messed up the one good babysitter we did have. It didn't take long before Versa was strung out on that stuff. Back to square one.

Our final babysitters were Laura and Chestine. They were best friends. Whenever you saw Laura, Chestine wasn't too far behind. The two seemed inseparable; it was like they were adjoined at the hip. They did everything to-gether, so my mom didn't mind Laura inviting Chestine over as long as she was attentive to my brother and me.

One day I called my mom complaining, "Mom they been in your room all day and me and Courtney haven't ate." My mom came home, walked into her bedroom and found Laura and Chestine naked in bed getting it ON. At the time, I didn't know what a lesbian was, but I never saw Laura and Chestine again.

Since my mom couldn't seem to find an appropriate sitter, I was promoted to the job. At the age of seven I cooked, cleaned, and helped raise my little brother. I missed a bulk of my childhood and matured quicker than my peers. While my friends were outside playing, I was inside planning the dinner menu for that night. You probably can't even imagine a second grader with so much responsibility, but whining about my single parent home was not an option. It was all about survival.

Even though crying about my single parent home wouldn't change the situation, I can't front like I wasn't pissed. Why the Hell I gotta be stuck in the house making fried chicken, dinner rolls, and macaroni and cheese when just outside my window, my friends were down there jumping Double Dutch, I thought to myself. I'm sweating over a hot ass stove while they playing outside. This is some BULLSHIT.

As a first born child, I exhibit every stereotype there is. I'm a planner and an organizer. I'm driven, ambitious and very independent. It seems as though overnight I was expected to grow up, get straight A's, keep my little brother in line, and always be the responsible one. At times it became exhausting.

I still do this today, but there are times when I realize I just need nurturing, just like I did when I was a little girl trying to get my mom to see me as a kid.

It's OK if you have things that you may feel are flaws in your character. Allow yourself to be a child again and forgive that child and the parent that was taking care of her. Humans don't come with manuals. Most of us just do the best we can.

How I spent my summer vacation

very year when it was time to go back to school, the first assignment we were usually instructed to write a "How I Spent My Summer Vacation" essay. And every year I came back with an interesting story to tell.

When I was five, my brother and I began traveling to Haynes, Arkansas to visit our grandparents for the summer. For three whole months, our mother enjoyed a much needed break while my brother and I left the inner city and ventured off to the rural south. At first we used to think that the country was boring. At our age, attending Sunday school and church, doing chores until we grew tired and getting numerous whoopings with a switch was not our idea of a good time. But eventually we got creative and even started looking forward to our summers down South.

Me and my brother used to bet each other about who would get the least amount of whoopings each summer. No matter how good we were, you couldn't survive a summer with my Grandma Naomi without being disciplined. Sometimes we would get a whooping for no reason at all.

When we asked our grandma why she was whooping us she would just simply announce in between licks, "I'm whooping you for all the times I didn't catch you." And looking back on it now, I still can't think of a single time when she didn't catch us in the act of doing something we had no business doing.

One time my brother Courtney, our cousin Akissi, and I attempted to start a fire by rubbing two sticks together. We got the bright idea from this camping movie and of course after one whole hour and a pile of sticks later we were unsuccessful. Then my brother got a bright idea.

"I know we can start a fire with matches. I saw Paw Paw use them to light his cigarettes." So with that said, Courtney ran in the house to grab the box of matches that were on the counter lying next to our grandfather's ash tray. I almost went through an entire box of matches before Courtney interrupted again.

"Hey, I saw Paw Paw use this part of the box." And with one strike of the match my brother did it. He dropped the lit match in the pile of sticks and horse hay we had complied. Before we knew it, the fire had gotten out of control.

Our grandparents were rocking back and fourth on the swing that hung between two big oak trees, and my uncle Lester was sitting at the picnic table across from them when he noticed the smoke signals in the air. He quickly ran over to put out the fire. After he got the flames under control our granny called all three of us over. We hung our heads low because we already knew what was coming next.

"Now y'all know y'all ain't got no business playing with matches, now get over to that tree and pick a switch." We slowly walked over to the switch tree and plotted amongst each other that we would grab the smallest one we could find. We came back to the swing where our grandma sat.

"Oh, you tried to go over der and get a lil one huh? That's oh-kay I got anotha one right here." She reached behind the tree and revealed the biggest switch I have ever seen in my life.

I started crying before she even made contact and I shimmied across the dusty rock road trying to get away. And for a tobacco chewing, sherbert ice cream eating, soap opera watching, house coat wearing, large feet having, switching from side to side when she walked woman, this old lady sure had a strong arm. After whooping all three of us she walked in the house and we were left sitting with our grandfather.

Paw-Paw explained in his calm, low tone, "You kids could have hurt yourselves or even burned down the house." And with that our grandpa grabbed his cane with his arthritis hands and slowly stood up from his seat on the swing and limped into the house after our grandma. After they left we all just sat silently on the swing nursing our wounds, but what had hurt worse than our whooping was disappointing our Paw Paw.

Out of our summers down South I can only recall my grandfather whooping me once. One day my Paw-Paw overheard me talking back to my grandma. I wasn't brave enough to say it to her face so I whispered it under my breath.

"Ugh, she gets on my last nerve. I can't stand her. Can't wait to go home." Well obviously, my whisper was in earshot of my grandpa because he picked up a switch and took me in the back bedroom. After he whooped me, he explained in his calm demeanor that I shouldn't be bad-mouthing my grandmother and that my language was inappropriate.

Within a few hours things were back to normal. Grandma was back complaining about us running in and out of the house. "You letting all my good air out," she yelled as she locked us outside until we promised to stay indoors. The mosquitoes sure did enjoy Chicago blood. We rubbed alcohol on our mosquito bumps and watched Wheel of Fortune with Grandma.

The summer had gone and went and it was time to go back to school. How many people in my class can say that they played basketball with a crate hanging from a tree or that they used the light off a lightening bug as earrings or that a pinecone and a stick were their equipment used for a baseball game?

Looking back, I can see that it was extremely important to the person I am today to have grown up in both worlds - the city and the country. I don't know if I fully appreciated it then, but the country allowed me to spend a lot of time outdoors - riding horses, swimming, camping and being balanced by nature. This is where I learned to wash clothes and hang them on a clothesline, water the fields which grew our food, and retrieve eggs from the hen house.

Doing the everyday mundane things that seem un-important is what helps us develop good habits. It teaches us discipline and grows us into well-rounded individuals.

Behind the wheel

I was eight years old when I learned to drive. My mother took me and my brother to the South Shore Beach parking lot and taught us how to drive in her gold '96 Mazda. I did good and maintained a slow and steady speed; my brother on the other hand, who was only six and thought he knew it all, jumped behind the wheel, which by the way he could barely see over, and put the petal to the floor. I screamed from the back seat and my mother hollered for him to slow down, but his foot was wedged underneath the gas pedal. The only thing that saved us that day from getting in a car accident was the speed bumps in the parking lot.

When we finally came to a screeching halt, my mother

threw the gear in park, exchanged seats with my brother and let out a deep sigh of relief. She didn't seem to notice the onlookers shaking their heads in utter disbelief. What in the world was she thinking, trying to teach two kids how to drive? She realized that just because she drove at a young age on the rocky dust roads down South didn't mean my brother and I should be allowed to drive in the city environment. The next time I got behind the wheel was eight years later when I took driver's education in high school.

> *I now look at my attempt at driving at such a young age as a metaphor for the rest of my childhood. Children should be allowed to grow up naturally and at their own pace. Don't thrust the weight of the world on them and place unrealistic expectation on their tiny shoulders. Let them be children. Let them play and use their imagination. Childhood doesn't last long, and they will have the rest of their lives to take on adult responsibilities.*

Brittany the bully

My brother and I went to O'Keeffe Elementary. We were both in advanced classes and got straight A's. Not because we wanted to, but we wanted our mom to have one less thing to worry about. She had enough on her plate. My mom was a lenient parent. I didn't have many rules to follow growing up. But then again, I didn't need any. I was very mature and responsible for my age. I implemented rules for my younger brother to follow. He had to do his homework before he played outside, clean his room at least twice a week and take out the trash when it got full. I took care of the rest which included cleaning our two bedroom apartment and cooking dinner. He played outside until the street lights came on, and then he would gobble down whatever I prepared.

On occasion I was interrupted from my household chores to help my brother fight. If you had a beef with my brother then you had a beef with me, and if you wanted to fight him, you damn sure was gonna have to scrap with me. See my mother taught us that if one fights then you both fight. Our family of three vowed to always look after one another. We stuck together because we were all we had. We were down for each other because that's how we were raised.

We moved around a lot during our childhood. It seemed like every year we were moving to a new neighborhood and making new friends all over again. We had just got settled in one place and just like that we had to move again. It was always hard to meet new people and leave our friends behind but we didn't have a choice.

One particular neighborhood that we ended up staying in for quite some time was 69th and Paxton. "Pax-town" was where we spent the bulk of our childhood days. There was a neighborhood tormenter who went by the name "Brittany the Bully." Everyone was scared of her and she knew it. She took advantage of everyone and if she wanted something that you had, she would just take it. My mother had taught me not to fear anyone, but Brittany wasn't just anyone. She was twice my size and four years older than me. She failed school three times and it didn't seem to bother her one bit.

When I moved into the neighborhood, I found out that she had a major crush on this boy named Juicy. The only problem was Juicy liked me. I couldn't help it if he was feeling me and not her. He wasn't my boyfriend, well not yet at least.

On this particular summer day, he rode his bike by me and said "Hey Ce, watch this." My new friends and I watched him do several tricks on his bike and I couldn't help but feel special because I knew that the cutest boy in the neighborhood was showing off for little `ole me. I guess Brittany noticed too and she definitely didn't like the attention he was giving me. She intimidated everyone, including me because today I was her chosen victim. I ran in the house crying to my mother.

"She is trying to beat me down Ma, Brittany the Bully is trying to beat me down." My mother's words have stuck in my head ever since that hot summer day.

"Cierra, you better get your ass out there and fight because if you don't stand up to her, I will beat your ass myself." So I turned around and went back outside to face Brittany. I had been whooped by my mother before and I was almost certain that any beating I got from Brittany could not compare.

We stood in the middle of a circle of kids who instigated the fight. I guess us arguing was not entertaining enough because I remember one girl getting between us and holding out her hands. Brittany hit her hand first and the next thing I know the girl in the middle punched me in my arm. I quickly caught on that the "hand game" was equivalent to Brittany getting the first lick. Naturally I passed the second hit and continued the game. How we eventually started fighting, I can't recall, but the next thing I recollect was Juicy and his brother breaking the fight up.

I looked down and saw four of my dookie braids lying on the ground. I looked at Brittany disgusted that she had pulled out my hair, but she was in far worst shape. She had a black eye forming and her mouth was full of blood. My knees were scratched and some of my hair was pulled out, but I survived. Everyone crowded around me bragging about how I was the winner. I was just glad that I had defended myself.

From that day on, Brittany never messed with me again! I guess I had earned her respect and I promised myself that I would never allow another person to bully me again. We continued to move a great deal, but at least now it was in the same neighborhood. We found apartments on the same exact block, sometimes around the corner. We didn't need a moving truck or even professional movers, all of our friends would pitch in as we carried furniture down the street above our heads. My brother and I were happy that we were finally able to keep and maintain friendships.

There will always be people who will try to steal your joy by intimidating, bullying, controlling, or degrading you in some way. Standing up for what you believe is an important part of being an individual, but confrontation can be terrifying. Defend yourself and those who cannot defend themselves, but don't go looking for trouble. Be assertive but not aggressive. Be honest and direct, but be kind. Remain confident and firm in your beliefs and in this way, you will earn respect.

Stop, drop and roll

One day that I will never forget was when my brother set our room on fire. I was talking on a three way phone call while my younger brother watched The Fresh Prince of Bel-Air in our bedroom. All of a sudden I remember him going back and fourth from the kitchen to the bedroom with bowls of water. When I asked what he was doing with those bowls, he lied.

"I'm 'bout to drink this." I thought it was a bit strange, but was too consumed in my phone conversation to pursue the matter any further. His next words were, "HELP CIERRA" as the shadow of the blazes appeared on the wall. I dropped the phone, ran into our room, and was shocked to see that it was on fire. I quickly told him to get pots and buckets of water while I called my mother.

"Mom, Courtney caught our room on fire!"

"What! I'm on the way. Call 911!"

I quickly made the call, gave them our address and tried to aid my brother in controlling the flames. A next door neighbor knocked on the door and asked if we were okay because he smelled smoke, and my brother quickly lied to get rid of him.

"We 're okay. My sister just burnt dinner."

When the fire department arrived, they told us to get downstairs immediately. After they put the fire out, I was approached by a fireman who asked me all type of questions.

"How did the fire get started?" and "Where is your mother?" he inquired.

"She's at work so I'm babysitting my younger brother."

"You look to young to be looking after your little brother." I knew he would quiz me. "How old did you say you were again?"

Fourteen, Sir."

"What year were you born?" See right there, he thought he had caught me in a lie, but I also had my year of birth memorized to make me old enough.

"I was born in 1984," I answered.

Just then my mom came sprinting around the corner. She still worked for Cook County, but now she was an intensive probation officer. She had on her badge, gun, and vest. She had run 10 city blocks just to get to us. After seeing that we were okay, she rested her hands on her knees. The officer spoke briefly with her and then she pulled us aside.

The first question that came out of her mouth was, "How old did you tell them you were?"

"I told them I was fourteen just like we practiced." My mom taught me that at the age of eleven I could not legally look after my brother and that I had to be at least fourteen to be considered a babysitter.

After hearing my response she let out a quick sigh of relief and cried, "I thought that they were gonna take my babies away from me."

After the fire had been put out, I stood there looking at my burnt bed lying on the ground. I questioned my brother and he finally revealed that he was playing with a lighter and wanted to see if the straw underneath my bed would burn. He quickly gained knowledge that straw bums pretty fast. He should have known that much from our down South experience.

Why couldn't he experiment on his bed, I wondered. A.J., our friend who lived in the building, started joking about the incident.

"Where are you going to sleep now, Cierra?"

I hit him in his arm and shrieked, "Shut-up. This isn't funny." Then we all laughed, my mother included. I think she was just glad that we were alright.

That was literally the last straw, I complained about getting my own room. I was getting to old to be sharing one with my little, annoying brother. I guess my mom was also ready for a change because she started shopping for a house the very next day.

> *When we really think about what's important, I've learned that the simple answer is "family". Family is important. Make your family and the people who are most important to you, people who are like fam-*

ily, the most important thing in your life. Stand by them even when they make mistakes. Show them you can be counted on to be there for them in good times and bad. Don't take loved ones for granted, and most of all, forgive them in the same way you want to be forgiven for your mistakes. Love them, no matter what comes.

The deal fell through

One day our mother told us that she had found a home and that we would be moving. My brother and I got all excited and bragged to all of our friends. Well, we should have kept our mouths closed because we were embarrassed when we did not move.

We asked why we had not moved yet and she just replied, "The deal fell through." This 'moving into a house' business went on for years and my brother and I never seemed to learn our lesson. Every time our mother told us we were moving, we would go off and get all excited, but after three years and eight 'moves', we gave up and stopped believing our mother about getting a house. Ironically, the time when she really meant it, my brother and I didn't even seem to care. We were tired of being overjoyed and then let down. Our mother assured us that she had found a home in the suburbs and that we were really moving this time, but we did not believe her until she came and transferred us out of school. This was when we realized that she was serious this time.

It seemed like we rode in the car for hours to get to our home in the suburbs, although my mom insisted that it was only thirty minutes away. During the long ride, I finally realized that a new home also meant a new school and new friends. After thinking about it for a while, moving to a new house didn't seem all that great. I was leaving my friends behind and I wasn't ready for that. My thoughts were interrupted when we pulled up in front of a two story brick house in the suburb of South Holland. My mouth dropped and my eyes popped out of my head. My brother and I sprinted inside the gigantic house and ran up and down the flights of stairs. I had never had my own room before. My privacy was always non-existent sharing a room with my annoying sibling. But I would no longer have that problem.

Moving to a new home can be unsettling, but realize that everything happens for a reason. I wasn't sure I wanted to move from the city to the suburbs, but I trusted my mom to know what was best for us. I knew she wanted a better life for all of us, and she never lost her vision of the American Dream - the house with the white picket fence, the two car garage, and the neighborhood cookouts in the backyard.

Never lose sight of your dream. Focus ever-increasing amounts of energy on what you want and eventually, it will become a reality.

Product of your environment

My mother was offended when we transferred into our new school, McKinley Junior High because the administration asked to see our previous records to make sure that we were not gang members. My mother was highly upset that the school principal automatically assumed that we were gang affiliated because of the neighborhood we had come from. I grew up on the South-East side of Chicago in a poor, minority neighborhood and attended a school where gang activity, drug use, and disorderly conduct were the norm.

Despite all of this, my mother assured the school administration that we were not your stereotypical kids from the hood. Neither my brother nor I had ever been in a gang and our grades, school attendance, and reputation were excellent. She slammed our previous report cards on the desk and after reviewing them, they did not seem to be impressed, even though we excelled in our gifted programs. They looked her straight in her eyes and suggested that we start off in regular classes because their curriculum was more intense.

"They can handle the work," my mother assured them, but they did not budge. My morn was upset because of the way they looked down on us. That night she took us home and explained to us that we had to make it evident to everyone that they shouldn't judge a book by its cover, especially after skimming through the pages and writing you off without a second thought.

The next day my brother and I went to school with a new found determination that we would prove everyone wrong. We went to our 'regular classes' and did just that, proving that people should be judged by their actions, not their appearance, not their background and not their environment. After a week or so in class, both our teachers recommended that we be placed in advanced classes.

My brother was the class clown, but he knew all the answers when his teacher called on him. He was bored and he needed to be challenged. After our new placement, my brother and I could hardly wait to tell our mom.

"Mamma, guess what? They put us in gifted classes."

She seemed pleased but then replied, "Getting in the class is just half the battle." My brother looked baffled, but I understood completely. Now that we had been moved to the advanced classes, we had to prove that we belonged there. And just like that getting an 'A' was not good enough; I strived for an `A+`, the best grade in the class.

I competed with my peers in everything and I suppose that's why the coaches at the school thought that I would make a great athlete. They were shocked when they discovered that I had never played any sports. The only time I had ever showed interest in sports was when I was watching my crush shoot jumpers in his opponents' eyes.

They couldn't believe that at my height I had never played and they insisted that I at least try it out. My mother thought that it was a great idea for me to get involved with sports. This way I could make friends while still keeping my grades up because it was policy on the teams that "you had to make the grades to play."

I wanted to try out for the girl's basketball team, but I had got there too late and their season had already begun. So I tried out for volleyball and to my surprise, I made the squad. I couldn't even hit the ball over the net during tryouts but I suppose my coach saw major potential. I improved my game every practice and before long I could set, spike and serve the best on the team. At the end of the season I received the 'Most Improved Player Award.'

During the summer, a girl from the team asked me if I wanted to play basketball on her summer league team. Her dad, Mr. Russell, was the coach of the Lady Wildcats and he was impressed with my volleyball season. I was open and honest about my lack of experience but he assured me that I would be just fine. I worked really hard over the summer and came back with confidence my eighth grade year. I made the basketball team and for the first time in the school's history, we were undefeated.

I will always be grateful to Mr. Russell for allowing me to play for him and teaching me the basics of the game. I played volleyball that year, too, and we had another successful season. I wasn't the fastest person on the track team but I broke records in shot put and discus. By the time I graduated from McKinley Junior High School, I had a whole new circle of friends from playing volleyball, basketball and running track.

Outside of school I also was a member of Sweet Holy Spirit's step ministry where we evangelized and used step performances to minister to the youth. I was glad that we moved. My brother seemed happier than he had ever been and my mother was thankful that he found sports to be his extracurricular activity as well. When we moved from the inner city, he was right around the age when gangs snatched innocent boys and molded them into young thugs. He wouldn't become a victim to the streets and we were glad.

When we're young, we don't usually understand how our decisions can impact our lives. There are many temptations in life, and every decision you make, every step you take, will effect the way your life unfolds. Be conscious of your reality. Think before you speak or act. Don't just "go with the flow" because even that's a decision - a decision to do nothing. You are the only person who can choose the final direction of your life by the decisions you make.

High school summer league

Thornwood High School was the neighborhood high school in South Holland. All my friends and I went to Thornwood after graduating from McKinley. The summer before my freshman year, I participated in Thornwood's basketball summer league. The league was for incoming freshman through juniors in high school and the girls were split up into three squads: freshman, sophomore, and varsity.

I was still fairly new to the game of basketball; after all, I had only started playing one year prior. I heard about the league so I went to the practice on the first day. When I arrived, the girls were all ready split up into their separate teams and going through drills. I did not want to interrupt so I grabbed a seat in the bleachers. After about five minutes I saw a woman heading my way. She seemed pleasant, but stern. For a second, I thought that she was going to ask me to leave, but instead she simply sat down next to me and started talking.

"So, are you hear for our summer league," she asked?

"Yeah, one of my friends told me about it so I figured that I would come check it out."

"Well, why don't you join us?" she requested.

I was happy and nervous all at the same time. I followed her to the court where she introduced me to the team. I was so scared by this time that I was probably shaking. These girls were experts, in my opinion. They mostly were all in high school and competing on a higher level than me. They had grown up with a ball in their hands and here I was a rookie who was just getting started. Right before it was my turn to do the defensive drill they were working on, I saw a familiar face. It was my friend, Danae, who had invited me out. She smiled at me and I suddenly became more at ease. After a tough two hour practice, the coach pulled me aside and asked me if I would come back.

I felt relieved that I was able to keep up with the other

girls and quickly sputtered "Yes!"

She sent me home with a release form that my mother had to fill out. Also in the envelope was a paper that requested a fee for participating in the summer league. My mother was happy for me but I knew that she could not afford to pay the summer league fees. The next day I returned to the gym a little early to break the news to Coach. I gave her the release form and explained to her that my family could not afford to pay the fees.

I turned away to leave the gym when she yelled, "Wait, Cierra, we can waive the fees for the program."

I was ecstatic. I hugged the coach, said thank you, and sprinted into the hallway to call my mom. Ten minutes later, I returned to the gym right when the other girls were arriving.

That day we had a game and I was just finding out about it. Coach gave me a jersey and told us to load the vans. When we arrived to the game, the coach pulled me aside.

"I am impressed with how you played yesterday. I'm convinced that you could play on the sophomore squad."

I felt flattered, but was also caught off guard. I didn't even know that we had a game today and minutes before warm-ups the coach discloses that she wants to promote me to the sophomore team. I can tell that my mom was just as shocked when she saw me seated with the older girls. I watched from the bench for the first quarter while my coach hollered at the top of her lungs. The team wasn't doing so well.

The next thing I remember was Coach looking into my eyes and saying, "Okay Thurman, let's see what you got. Don't forget that you are going against sophomores now so you better not play like a freshman."

I was buzzed into the game and never came out. By the end of the fourth quarter the coach was impressed with my stats, 15 points, 7 rebounds, and 2 steals. The varsity girl's team congratulated me on the game and my performance, and the team went out for ice cream to celebrate our victory.

I will never forget this outing because this was the first time a female flirted with me. At first, I thought that she was simply being nice, but I soon realized that it was more when she attempted to caress my hand after I gave her a high five. I felt uncomfortable so I told my friend about the incident. She did not seem surprised at all; instead she sat down and explained to me that some of the girls on the team liked girls instead of boys. I thought back to our baby-sitters Laura and Chestine.

Awwww, so she's a lesbian, I thought. From that moment on, I knew I had to watch my back because every chance she got, she was flirting with me. Even after this experience I never labeled all female hoopers as homosexual. Although I have encountered a few, I don't feed into the stereotype.

The next day at practice, Coach sat me down to 'chat.' I braced myself because I had become accustomed to her 'chats' and they always ended up with shocking news. This time it was no different.

She came right out and said, "Thurman, I think you have the potential to play on Varsity. You could really help out the team."

I was stunned. This was a big move that I didn't think I was prepared for. I tried to sway her decision by explaining to her that I had just started playing basketball the previous year. She said that it did not matter when I started. She told me never to fear my talents but to embrace them. After talking with her, I was sent to play on the varsity squad for the remainder of summer league. My summer league career was a successful one and when the regular season began, I was starting on Varsity.

> *Life will present you with many challenges, some of which you may feel you're not ready to take on. Stretch yourself. Adjust your game plan and focus on the next play. You may be better or more capable than you realize.*

Goodbye means forever

My grandfather played a big part in my life and when he passed away a piece of me died, too. He was a lighthearted and wise man. He spoke in a slow and easy tone because he wanted people to understand every word that came out of his mouth. His words were strong, yet he never raised his voice. I hated disappointing him.

He was a very religious man. His Bible was always within arms reach. He sat on the first pew at church, taught Sunday school, was the head deacon on the deacon board, and was a soloist who was known for his distinguished style of singing "Till The Old Ship of Zion."

Born and raised in Arkansas, my favorite picture of him is the black and white photo of him dressed in his U.S. Navy uniform when he served in World War II. He was a carpenter by trade; he built the 3 bedroom-1 bath house he raised his family in. He worked in a metal factory until gout arthritis crippled his hands, while my grandmother worked as a cook in the kitchen of an old folk's home. I use to think she was a nurse because she wore an all white uniform, white tights and white shoes.

I was always impressed by him as a child because he always seemed larger than life. He told knock-knock jokes, rode us on his lap as he cut the grass, made a swing in between two big oak trees, and built us a red tricycle to ride. When we got too big for the tricycle it was passed on to the next generation and made a swing in between two big oak trees.

He always made me feel special. At dinner time, he sat at the head of the table and blessed the food as everybody joined hands and bowed our heads. He liked his coffee jet black with lots of sugar. He wore a gray grandfather's hat, kept a pack of Kool 100s cigarettes in his top shirt pocket and walked with a cane.

In the summer we would water the crops in the field with our Paw-Paw and help grandma hang the laundry on the clothes line in the back of the house.

He refused to let the doctors operate on him to remove the growth on the back of his neck that was cutting off his air supply. We visited him in the hospital and tears streamed down my face; I hated seeing him that way. I leaned over and kissed him on his head and he whispered in my ear. His voice was softer than usual.

"Baby, I'm tired."

"It's gone be okay Paw-Paw."

"I know Ce-Ce, cuz I got the Lord by my side," he replied. He wasn't afraid of death; the last words I recall him saying came from a verse in the King James Bible, Psalms chapter 90, verse 10:

"The days of our years are threescore years and ten."

For those of you unfamiliar with the Bible, a score is equivalent to 20 years and since we are promised 3 score you can do the math. 3 times 20 equal 60. But don't forget to add the 10. In other words, God promised man a life of at least 70 years and my grandfather was pleased because he had already surpassed that age. I prayed to God to let him stay, but I suppose the Lord had other plans. He passed away at 78. I was being selfish, I didn't want him to leave, but he was tired of suffering.

On October 28, 2001 Dessie Lee Brooks Sr. went home to be with the Lord. When it came to the point in the funeral service when the grandchildren reflected on our grandfather, we each stood up one by one sharing our fondest memory of him. Each reflection concluded with "I knew I was his favorite." Before long murmur spread amongst the grandchildren about who really was his favorite.

Finally, my Uncle James stood at the podium and announced, "He was a very special man; He had a unique way of relating and communicating with everyone he met, which led others to love, respect and admire him. He made everybody feel like they were his favorite."

He was buried on Clay Hill in the cemetery down the road from my Grandma Naomi's home. The grave site is parallel to the pond where all ten of his children were baptized: Dessie Lee Jr., Danny, Birdie Mae (Mae Mae), James, Verlean (Pee Wee), Deborah, Lester, Larry, Joe Ann, and Rose (Robin). The memories of him that each of us holds dear will definitely be cherished by his wife, 10 children,

25 grandchildren, 20 great-grandchildren, and a host of nieces, nephews, cousins and friends. I know he is looking down on me, he will truly be missed. Family reunions will never be the same.

> *Happiness is a decision you make in life. Life is full of so much potential, and how we view the world will either make or break us. My grandfather always chose to be happy and you can, too. Don't wait to find the goodness in life. Find it now. Tomorrow is a day that never comes and all the happy 'todays' you create will become happy memories. Choose to be happy today and you will spread happiness to others, who will pass it on, making the world a better place for all of us.*

Hoop dreams

asketball is a physical sport so injuries are a part of the game. Looking at my reflection in the mirror you can barely notice my high school basketball battle wounds.

On one occasion, while going up for a rebound, I caught a nasty elbow and still have a light scar above my right eyebrow from the stitches (8 to be exact) that I had to get. Oh, and this one time I got hit in the mouth busting through a screen and after a few days a bump formed on my upper lip and never went away. My nose was even broken while playing against one of our conference team rivals, Thornton. I had to wear a protective face mask and my nose is still crooked to this day.

I remember how upset I was about wearing the mask. It hindered my vision and made the game of basketball much more difficult. I played four games in the mask before becoming so frustrated that in the middle of a play I just slung it over to my team's bench. I celebrated the return of my peripheral vision by surpassing the 1,000 point barrier to my career.

As a four-year starter playing major minutes, it was only a matter of time before I scored 1,000 career points. I finished that game with 16 points, 8 rebounds and 4 steals in less than three quarters.

Another moment that sticks out about my high school basketball career was when we, the Thornwood Thunderbirds, played the Homewood Flossmoor Vikings in the conference championship game. The gym was packed to capacity as we battled back and fourth with our toughest competitors. West Virginia University-bound center and future WNBA Detroit Shock draft pick, Olayinka Sanni, poured in 14 points and grabbed 11 rebounds for the Vikings. With less than three seconds left on the clock, and my team down by one in the fourth quarter, I was sent to the line to shoot two free throws. Talk about the weight of the world on your shoulders, well at least the weight of the SICA East Conference.

Throughout my basketball career, my coaches had given me suggestions to create a routine that helped me concentrate and knock down my free throws. Right now, my ability to make these two free throws would contribute to the win or loss for my team. I had 20 points and 19 rebounds, but I had been shooting worse than Shag from the line.

I stepped up to shoot my first free throw as my mom shushed loud and crazy fans. I said a quick prayer before stepping up to the line. I bent my knees, dribbled the ball two times in front of me and once to the side before shooting the ball. The first shot went in. The crowd exploded but I remained focused.

"Okay girl, your job ain't done yet," I whispered to myself. I had never faced this kind of pressure before. The fate of the game rested in my hands. I stepped up to the line for a second time, performed my routine and swish, nothing but net. The crowd went wild. My teammates quickly picked up full court on defense. H-F barely got the ball in play before reaching the 5 second penalty. They took a few dribbles but couldn't get a shot off in time. As the time expired, my teammates rushed me on the court. I couldn't believe it; we beat Homewood-Flossmoor in the conference championship game.

Those were the biggest free throws I have ever had to make in my life. I finished my high school basketball career with 1,227 career points, ranking as the third all-time scorer, and grabbed 744 rebounds, breaking the school record. Not bad for a girl who didn't grow up with a ball in her hands and didn't start hooping until 8th grade.

When it comes to the game of life, just like basketball, take time to breathe. Celebrate your victories and be thankful for all that you're capable of.

My firsts

When I think back to my list of first time experiences, they were, for the most part, worthwhile and rewarding. Others however were quite uneventful.

I was nine years old when I had my first kiss. My friends and I were playing "Catch a girl, Kiss a girl." I ran off quickly once the game began, but slowed my pace once I realized that the cutest boy in the school was closing in on me. When he caught me, he bragged, "I got you Cierra."

I replied back, "So, what that mean?" I knew exactly what it meant and I was anxious for him to lay one on me.

"That means we gotta kiss now."

"Ok, I guess," I smacked my lips as if I didn't really want to feel how soft his were.

We kissed and the next day, the cutest boy in the school was my first boyfriend. It lasted all of two weeks, which is appropriate for a couple of fourth graders.

I was 15 years old when I went on my first date. Well actually it was a double date with my best friend, Victoria. We met the guys at the River Oaks Mall in the food court. After we met up, we walked to the movie theatre near the entrance of the mall. I can't remember what we saw that night, but I do recall my date buying me a medium sized popcorn and medium drink. I hated the white movie popcorn drizzled in butter and salt. I would have much rather preferred some store bought hot or cheese popcorn, but I thanked him and shared it with him anyway. I made a mental note to bring my big purse next time filled with my favorite snacks.

My friend and I sat in the middle of our dates and at the end of the movie we window shopped in the mall until my mom came to pick us up. My date kissed me on the cheek and I waved him goodbye. I ran to my mother's truck, hoping and praying that she had not seen us.

Another first time that sticks out in my mind was my first car, a sky blue hooptie Honda that my mother's friend sold to me for one buck. I had just concluded Driver's Ed so I was excited to have my very own car. When my friends rode with me, they had to pay two dollars for gas money. Public transportation wasn't free and neither was I.

I held that car together pretty well. I kept it clean, changed the oil on time and always had at least a half tank of gas. When I went away to college, I left the car at home so my brother could drive it. I never saw my Honda again. Courtney never changed the oil, gas tank stayed empty, and drove on a doughnut on a daily bases.

So far I've talked about my first kiss, first boyfriend, first date and my first car, now its time to reveal my very first sexual encounter. I sat down next to my mom on the living room couch. Well, actually it was called the family room; we are not allowed to enter the living room because it's just there to "look pretty." The attractive room had hardwood floors, a living room set in pretty shades of cream and peanut butter, and a glass table which served as a center piece. A crystal chandelier adorned the ceiling and a single portrait of a daughter sitting on her mother's lap decorated the otherwise plain white walls.

Once a week my mother dusted the Italian leather furniture and swept the hardwood floors. I'm uncertain why because there was never a trace of dust or dirt in the living room. I suppose the fact that my younger brother and I have been banished from within its four walls keeps it pretty tidy. The family room on the other hand, is where we all used to hang out. When my brother wasn't playing video games in his room or I wasn't talking endlessly on the house phone, the family room was our place to gather.

Usually after dinner we sat down as a family and watched television. Sometimes we popped in a movie or played board games; but whatever the activity was, we do it together as a family.

On this particular night, my brother was staying overnight at his best friend's house. My mom and I sat side by side watching my favorite sitcom, Girlfriends. We laughed at how silly Joan looked dressed in a sombrero and long flowing skirt for the Mexican holiday, Cinco de Mayo. Joan was this highly educated, overly organized, never break the rules, uptight woman out of her circle of friends. She loved hosting parties no matter what the occasion. So when her girlfriends declined to celebrate Chico de Mayo, Joan threw a sombrero over her puffy hair in hopes of boosting their holiday spirits. The moment Joan began her ridiculous song and dance performance, we burst out laughing.

On the commercial break I asked my mom, "How can you tell if you are ready to loose your virginity?"

She muted the big screen TV, looked me dead in my eyes and replied, "If you have to ask then you are probably not ready."

She listened to me discuss my relationship with my boyfriend and how "all my friends are doing it." She assured me that they are not all sexually active and asked, "Are you being pressured?"

"No, MOM, I think I'm ready," I revealed.

"Cierra, once you loose your virginity, you can't get it back" she restates. "But if you think you are ready, then tomorrow we will go to the doctor and get you some birth control pills." The next day we did just that.

Even after we got the birth control, my mom still tried to convince me, "It might be best that you wait, there is no rush." At sixteen I thought I knew it all. I'm practically grown and my boyfriend loves me, I thought. So despite my mother's advice, I still decided to have sex.

After I did it, I wished I would have waited. It felt like someone was ripping my inside out.

"Are you okay," my boyfriend asked as he lay on top of me. "I'll go slow. You don't want me to stop do you?"

Shaking my head I responded, "I'm ok; you don't have to stop."

Two minutes later, he stopped anyway. First, he started breathing really heavy, and then he let out a sigh before collapsing on top of me. That's it, I thought.

Looking back on it now, I'm certain my boyfriend didn't have a clue about what he was doing either. I wish I could waive a magic wand and get my virginity back. My boyfriend and I broke up shortly after. I finally understood what my mom had been trying to explain. I finally realized that I was not ready to have sex. I waited an entire year and a half before I did "IT" again.

Don't allow peer pressure or the desire to be accepted and liked make you do something you know is wrong for you. I slept with my boyfriend because I was trying to find love and self-worth in the wrong way. I wanted to please him, and instead of bringing us closer together, having sex actually fast-tracked us to the demise of the relationship. Instead of a win-win it was a lose-lose.

Momma

My mom decided she didn't need a traditional real estate agent to sell her two-story home in South Holland. After all, her step daughter had been in the business for years and it seemed to be a pretty good idea to enlist her professional help. She wanted to maximize her profits any way possible so my mother hired my big sister to sell her house. Within a month, my sister had several interested buyers. The home-buyers who stood out were supposedly a couple from Shaunta's church, and my sister guaranteed that my mom would walk away with at least $20,000 from the transaction.

At the time, my mother was unaware that my sister had drafted two separate documents listing different prices. At the time, my mother didn't know Shaunta's real reason in discouraging her from getting a lawyer. At the time, my mother was unaware that the buyers, their real estate agent and my sister were all in a secret pact to profit from the sale of my mother's home. The system was rigged to sweeten the deal for everyone except my mom.

During the closing, my sister started coming up with all these unexpected expenses. Not only did the burden fall upon my mom to pay the unexpected fees, but she had less than 30 days to move. My mom walked away from the deal with $5,000, but Shaunta had gotten well over $28,000. No one said Shaunta shouldn't make money from the deal, but it was a shame that she decided to rip off my mom in the process.

Mom had planned on moving into a house in Chicago, but that deal fell through. With no other option, she moved us into an apartment in Calumet City.

Despite all she's been through, she continues to praise the Lord. I discovered some interesting things about my mom while talking with her co-workers.

First, I interviewed Charles Stiggers, a fellow probation officer who has known my mom for more than seven years.

He is stylish in his silk black shirt, brown business pants and Stacey Adams shoes. He wears a gold bracelet, gold watch, and gold wedding ring. He looks me straight in my eyes with his designer, prescription eye glasses and complains about my mother being "too nice." Giving bus fare or lunch money to their clients crosses the line.

"Your mom will go in her pocket and give them some money so they can get to where they need to go," exclaimed Mr. Stiggers. He blames her southern roots for her caring personality.

Veronica Robinson, on the other hand, thinks its God's presence in her life that shines through. Veronica is short and overweight with salt and pepper hair. She expresses her initial concern with being the "new girl" (two years ago) and reveals that she prayed to meet someone who would help her at her new job. The first person she met was my mother. "Thank you, Jesus," was the first words that came out of Veronica's mouth. Here Veronica describes how my mom greeted her.

"Girl, come on in here. What you doing sitting out here in this lobby? What desk you want? Pick a desk." When Veronica inquired about the desk by the window, my mom announced that she can have any desk she wanted. Next she cleaned the desk off, hooked up the computer for her, and showed her the supply closet. Veronica thought to herself that the Lord had answered her prayers and sent her an angel.

Even her co-worker, Nicolas Holmes, recognizes her strength. Nick is the youngest probation officer at their job. He is extremely attractive at 27 and looks very handsome dressed in all black. He wears a black, long sleeve, button down business shirt, black slacks, and black Steve Madden shoes. He sports a silver watch and a silver bracelet. His thick eyebrows lay down smoothly and his dimples appear when he smiles.

Nick revealed that my mom is easy to talk to, down to earth, and that he admires her for the type of parent she is.

"We talk about everything. I have five aunts and I'm probably closer to her than I am to any of them," whispered Nick.

Looking at her today, you would not be able to tell that she survived so much. The stove top, which is covered in alumina foil, is safe from splashing grease. The entire apartment fills with the aroma of sausages, eggs, cheese, and butter milk biscuits. She walks over to the refrigerator in her slippers; she refuses to walk bare foot on any floor surface. Her hair is half curled and half straight with a hot pink rat-tooth comb sticking out the side. She does not wear makeup, partly because she believes in natural beauty and partly because her mom never taught her how to apply it. But with her coco butter soft skin, she does not need any help enhancing her beautiful features. She stands at 5'5" with high cheekbones and a smile that could brighten any room.

She still wears her ten year old Mickey Mouse Christmas pajama top that comes just above her knees. Further down her left calf is a tattoo of a butterfly sitting on a rose. She still can not believe that my younger brother and I talked her into getting it.

We eat breakfast, while our dog Smokey begs to be fed from the table. He is a gray and white shih-tzu with the biggest brown eyes I have ever seen. I ignore him for as long as I can before I give in and sneak him a bite size piece of my sausage. My mom didn't like me feeding the dog from the table, but how could I resist him with his head tilted slightly down and his eyes looking up like he is about to cry. She didn't see me feed him table scraps because she was busy washing the dishes.

I remember when my mother first got Smokey from her ex-boyfriend, France. France's friend was moving into a condo and because of the no pets allowed rule, he wanted to find the dog a good home.

"Later on that day, France came over to the house with the dog and when I first saw him, he ran and jumped up on me and started wagging his tail," she recalls of their initial meeting. Smokey won her over right away and he raised the stakes once my mom discovered that he was already house broken.

She called bragging to me one day. "Cierra, girl he don't pee in the house."

She told me about her first experience walking the dog. She was thrilled when he walked up to a tree and hunched up his leg. His next designated spot was the fire hydrant, and then the bushes on the corner. He peed like twenty times marking his territory, a little squirt here and a little squirt there. Finally, he boo-booed and attempted to kick dirt over it with his hind legs.

Seven moving boxes are stacked by the back door. Even

though we have lived here for a year now, she still has not gotten around to unpacking. She does not want to get too comfortable, after all this "apartment thing was only suppose to be temporary."

My mother has persevered through a stroke at the age of 17, the death of her first husband, an abusive second husband turned bigamist, conniving scheming family members who have ripped her off, and has single handedly raised two kids. She is more than a mother to me, she is my best friend.

> *It seems the older I get, the smarter my mother seems to have been (and still is). They say youth is wasted on the young, and now I know why. We need to listen to our parents when we're children so we can learn from their experience. They don't tell us things just to hear themselves talk.*

A change in plans

*S*itting on the living room couch with my head rested on my hand, I stare aimlessly at the 42 inch flat screen mounted on the wall. Sitting between my legs is my doggie, Smokey. He follows me wherever I go. When I move, he moves. If I put on my coat or grab my keys, he knows that we are going outside. He loves the outdoors. He keeps a smile on my face. He is like my little baby. Sometimes I hold him in my arms and rock him to sleep while rubbing his tummy.

I remember the first time he slept in my room when I came home from school. I was in my bed when all of a sudden I heard this loud sound coming from the foot of the bed. I looked down onto the floor and there Smokey was, lying on his back, paws straight up in the air, snoring like a grown man without a care in the world.

Over the years, I've grown accustomed to this nightly nuisance and now it doesn't bother me one bit. I can sleep peacefully with Smokey all night long. My mom will admit that she is jealous of the relationship I have with Smokey.

"You just came and took my dog, " she complains. "I don't think he knows I am his rightful owner."

I giggle at her miniature temper tantrum and reply, "He's belongs to both of us." But the truth of the matter is, once I got out of school, Smokey started spending more time with me. I am the one who feeds him. I am the one who walks him. I take him to be groomed. I play with him throughout the day. I take him shopping for new clothes and toys. My mom bathes him, but I am the one who blow dries and brushes his hair. I am the one who sprinkles baby powder on his fur. So naturally he sees me as his master. He greets me at the door when I come home.

"Heeeeeeey, man, how my baby been doing today," I babble in my best baby voice. Smokey can tell I am happy to see him because he prances over to his toy squeaky dog bone.

There have been other times though when I had to punish him. He can tell I am upset by the pitch and tone in my voice. He tries to hide underneath my bed when I beckon him to his cage for peeing on the floor. I can't stay upset with him for too long though because his big brown eyes look up at me apologetically and I cave. So for the most part, I just leave the enforcing up to my mom.

Lounging around in my sweatshirt and jogging pants is becoming routine. Not by choice of course. I'd much rather be sitting at a desk in some office suited and booted, or maybe even teaching in an urban public school, but what's a college graduate to do when the job offers just aren't rolling in? My friends and family try to keep my spirit lifted.

"Girl, we are in a recession. Something's gonna come through. You just have got to be patient and trust in GOD." I guess they're right but this wasn't supposed to happen to me. It wasn't supposed to happen like this. I had a plan, you know, I always have one. But unfortunately graduating from Loyola University with a job already lined up didn't happen, contrary to my plan. Everyone thought I would be playing in the WNBA or overseas.

I, on the other hand, never saw a professional basketball career in my future. It wasn't a military secret that my mom couldn't afford to send me to college so I had to devise a plan. It worked out too; I graduated number five from Thomwood High School with a full ride to Loyola University.

> *Plans are great, but what I've come to learn is that plans can change. Life can force you to make a change in your well-laid plans. Now, at 28, I sometimes tell myself I should be married, have a family, and received a promotion. I should have, could have, would have been a lot of things by now if...Sometimes we have to abandon our plans and relieve the pressure we put on ourselves. Realize that there are things in life you can't control and that maybe God has a bigger plan for you.*

Recruiting 101

The basketball recruiting process was great. I didn't realize I was such a hot commodity until I started going on my recruiting visits. Colleges were treating me like royalty all because they wanted me to play basketball for their school.

My most memorable college campus visit was at Alabama State University. My mother accompanied me on the trip. There was no way she was missing out on all the perks.

The Assistant Women's Basketball Coach picked us up from the airport and escorted us to the University. First, I met the head coach and my potential future teammates who took me on a tour of the school. After the tour, my mother and I checked into our luxury hotel suite, which by the way was equipped with a bedroom that was separated from the living area, as well as at least two bathrooms, a private kitchen, secluded balcony, and whirlpool tub.

We barely had time to unpack before we were out the door and headed to the football game where the crowd dressed in black and gold represented the Hornets to the fullest. The crazed fans cheered just as loud during half-time as they did during the game, while the school band performed their routine.

No parents were allowed to the campus party that followed the victory. I love to dance so I fit right in with the dread headed, gold grill-mouthed students. After the party, I went back to my room and got some much needed rest.

We ordered room service in the morning, then our tour guides ushered us back to campus where I watched the girl's team practice. I was impressed but knew I could make an immediate contribution to the team.

The next event was the county fair and then the movie theatre. After the show, we dined at my favorite restaurant, Red Lobster. A few of the Men's and Women's Basketball team members came over to my suite that night. I asked them a billion questions about the life of a college student-athlete. Before I traveled back home to Chicago, the head coach promised my mom that she would take good care of me. She knew my hesitation about going to school out of state.

I would miss my family, I would be homesick, and how would they get along without me? Should I stay or should I go? I sat down and wrote a pro/con list for comparing Alabama State and Loyola. It was a tough decision to make and in the end I chose to stay in Chicago. I decided to go to Loyola because it was close to home. My mother is my biggest fan so it was important to me that she still be able to come see my games. I also knew that I would receive an excellent education from this top ranked university.

Looking back though, I think I made my decision to attend Loyola too quickly. I should have given the offers from other schools (Northern Illinois, Miami, Alabama State, and UIC among others) more consideration, especially after the coach who recruited me, Mary Helen-Walker, was fired. It was a sign; it was a way out that I wish I would have taken. I didn't know it then, but the next four years I would soon discover how difficult college life could be.

Sometimes, even with all the best plans and advice in place, we'll make the wrong decision. I chose the wrong college, but I learned a lot about myself there. I learned to deal with people I don't agree with; people who may not have my best interest at heart. It's important to know, after much thought, when to fold and move on and when to face the situation without running. Sometimes you just need to endure it.

I'm sorry, Cierra

In my freshman year of college my team was playing in a Florida tournament and I was having the game of my life. I had scored a quick 12 points when we were on a three-on-two fast break when my teammate made a bad pass. My momentum was going forward and I planted and twisted my knee while tying to save the ball from going out of bounds. I heard this loud pop and instantly fell to the floor screaming, "A WWWWWWH-HHHHH."

My coach rushed on the court and kneeled down beside me. "Just breathe, Cierra, it's going to be okay. Try to calm down."

I continued to scream while holding my left leg, "MY KNEE, MY KNEE, I heard it pop." The gym fell completely silent but then started to clap once I was helped to my feet. Chris, the athletic trainer, and one of my teammates helped me to the bench. I was terrified of what just happened.

"Ce, I bet you tore your ACL," uttered Marquise, the team's point guard."

"Shut up, don't say that!" I shouted back. During half time, I saw the team doctor. He performed several knee tests then left me lying on the table. I saw him walk across the room and whisper in Chris's ear.

Why couldn't he just tell me what was wrong? Why did he just leave me here without saying anything? He's whispering to her. is it really that bad? These were all questions that rushed through my mind. Finally, after what seemed like an eternity (probably more like 60 seconds), Chris walked over to the training table. I wondered if she could see the fear in my eyes.

"Cierra, the doctor thinks you tore your ACL."

I stared at her with my mouth wide open, tears streaming down my face. "Chris don't...don't tell me that.

Please, please don't tell me that Chris," I sobbed shaking my head.

Chris tried to reassure me. "We can't be certain until we travel back home and get the MRI."

After she broke the news to me, I didn't know what to do. So I just laid there until the end of the game. She looked back at me as she walked out the room.

"I'm sorry Cierra."

> *Life can turn on a dime. Up to this point, I lived and breathed basketball, and with one wrong move, in an instant, it was gone. I had to change my perspective and my plans again, but I learned a valuable lesson - how to cope with frustration.*

Adversity builds character

An MRI performed one week later confirmed that I had torn my left anterior cruciate ligament and damaged my bone. My ACL was reconstructed from part of my hamstring. Rehabbing my knee was a painful process. Initially, my mobility was nonexistent and I suffered from a loss of independence. Tasks I usually performed without a second thought became a chore. I hated waking my mother up in the middle of the night to give me my pain medication. I felt useless!

Once I was able to return to school, a bulk of my rehab focused on strengthening my hamstring and leg muscles. When I returned to the court, I was apprehensive and scared out of my mind of re-injuring my knee. I was afraid of re-tearing my ACL or damaging something else. Through it all I received encouragement from my trainer, teammates, assistant coaches and my mother to be strong and stay positive. With their help, I regained a new mind set.

Rehab had always been my number one priority, but instead of just focusing solely on the physical aspect, I began to strengthen my mind. I now realized that in order to rehab back from this injury, I had to be mentally strong. Slowly I began to rebuild my confidence. I eased back into the flow of things and with each day became less nervous. I discovered a new found determination and everyone took notice. I was the first one to practice and the last one to leave the weight room.

I told myself over and over again that I could overcome this, and when I came back, I was ready to play. My head coach didn't think so, however. I was good enough to practice, but not good enough to play. I worked my ass off getting where I was. Rehabbing was a bitch, it was the most difficult and painful experience of my basketball career. I didn't think my head coach hated me, I knew she did. She did not recruit me so in her mind she was not obligated to play me. It didn't matter to her that I destroyed the starters she put in at every practice.

She yelled at every workout. "You gotta work for your playing time. No spots are guaranteed." Everyone in the gym including the assistant coaches knew that was a bunch of bullshit. I was putting her starters in the bucket and I still was riding the bench come game day. I never complained, worked my ass off in practice and proved that I deserved some playing time, but she refused to give me the opportunity.

The team was in last place in the conference so obviously her method wasn't working. She only played me when she was forced to play me due to her favorite players being in foul trouble. She wanted me to kiss her ass.

My mother told me when I was younger "Once you start kissing ass, you will be kissing ass for the rest of your life." Since I was not in the ass kissing business, she tried everything in her power to break me.

The only game that I stayed on the floor for a significant amount of time was my sophomore year when we played Youngstown State. As usual we were losing terribly. All of her front court players were in foul trouble. Coach really didn't want me to play; she even tried putting a guard in at the power forward position. Ever method failed so she had no option but to put me into the game.

I came off the bench and made an immediate contribution by scoring 15 points. Our opposing team didn't know I even existed. I wasn't even on the scouting report because I was always riding the bench. We went into the locker room at half time with the lead. Coach Reidy tried to congratulate me.

"Way to play, Thurman."

I know this. This ain't nothing new. I perform this way every practice.

You would assume that I would start the second half and keep the momentum going. Instead, once again she let her big fat ego get in the way of the team's success. I rode the bench the entire second half and we lost the game by one point. My team was disappointed and upset that Coach Reidy refused to play me after I did so well.

"She don't like me. I'm not bout to kiss her ass. I come to practice and get the job done. If she wanna keep losing that's on her," I told my team on the bus ride to the hotel.

There was no other explanation for her behavior. She

was trying to get me to leave and transfer schools. It got so bad that I almost did. After the game, I'd had enough. I went to Coach Barnes room to tell her that I was leaving.

"Coach, can I come in, I need to talk with you." "Yeah Ce, come on in." I could always talk to Coach Barnes, she always kept it real with me. She told me when I was right and she told me about myself when I was wrong. She was young and could relate to what I was experiencing because just a few years prior she had been in my position.

"You saw what happened today. It's obvious that she doesn't like me."

"Ce, I can't even lie, I can tell she's trying to break you down." I had heard her on the bench advocating for Coach Reidy to give me some playing time.

"Put Cierra in," she'd said. "Thurman can guard that girl." Each time Coach Reidy would walk down the bench in my direction and select someone beside me.

Coach Barnes knew how upset I was. We stayed up and talked almost two hours that night.

"She just might get what she wants because I am thinking about transferring schools."

"Wait a minute, Ce, you can't let her get to you. You

know what she's on. I know she makes things harder than what they have to be."

"Harder is an understatement Coach B. She's making my life a living hell."

"You're a leader on the team whether you play or not, what about your teammates."

"That's true, the team does need me."

"Just try to stick it out; I'm sure things will get better."

"What if it doesn't Coach?" "If it doesn't then we will reevaluate the situation at that time."

"Ok, I guess I can wait it out a little while longer."

I went back to my room that night with mixed emotions about why Coach B had encouraged me to stay. The irony in the story is that once we got back home from our road trip, Coach B pulled me aside and revealed that she would be resigning and going to coach at another school out of state.

"What you mean you leaving" I asked.

"Ce, I made the decision a long time ago."

"You convinced me to stay, and now you leaving. That ain't right Coach. Please don't leave me here with this lady. You know she crazy. You keep me sane in all this foolishness."

"I know you're upset but please try to understand my position." At first, I was really pissed off at Coach Barnes. How she gone tell me to stay and she leaving?

Later she told me her reason behind her madness. She did not want to tell me she was leaving, she knew that would sway my decision to leave and she wanted me to make my own mind up. She wanted me to be sure that was something I was ready for.

After Coach Barnes quit, the other coaches were right behind her. First I lost the coach who recruited me, now all three assistant coaches were leaving. They had gone to other programs. I was miserable, but it's not like I could blame them either. They had to do what they had to do.

There was a lot of shit going on behind closed doors that the people on the outside were unaware of. Plain and simple, Coach Reidy was the common denominator. She had on more than one occasion been accused of being a racist and she let her emotions and personal feelings about her players interfere with what was best for the team. How she got the position of a Head Coach in the first place still surprises me to this day. More assistant coaches were hired and quit after a few months.

Things got worse over the next two years. I ended up tearing both my menisuces and went through my second knee surgery. At least this time, I knew what to expect.

After her fourth loosing season, Coach Reidy was fired. I didn't even feel sorry for her one bit either. When I was a little girl, my mother used to always tell me that "adversity builds character." Well, if that's true, then my "character" has definitely been getting quite the workout. The way I look at it, everything worked out in my favor because I still graduated with honors and did it on Loyola's dime.

> *Through my basketball career, I learned how to apply hard work and dedication, and how to persevere when times get tough. I learned how to sacrifice for the greater good. Though my competitive nature was strong, I learned how to respect authority even when I didn't agree with their methods, and this has helped me greatly in the real world and in the position I hold today.*

Little known facts

I've always been tall for my age, which proved to be a source of insecurity for me growing up. In grammar school I hated being teased and beckoned to stand at the end of the 'shortest to tallest' line.

When I started dating in high school, I refused to wear heels. I knew they would make me taller than the boy so I opted for flats instead. It wasn't until I got to college that I started to wear heels. I started off with wedges then graduated to kitten pumps. Now I will wear 4 inch heels without a second thought. I use to be self conscious about my height, you probably would be too if you stood 5'11 in socks, but since I can't change it, I've learned to embrace it.

People say that if you are tall then you should either play basketball or model. I say, "Why can't I do them both." If you see me on the court, I'm hooping like a straight up dude; but after the game you can catch me switching out the locker room. Most likely I'm rocking some sweats and probably my brown head scarf, but no one could tell me I wasn't fly.

My ex used to rap, so along the way I picked up a few skills. Check out my flow.

"Yeah, I see you looking, hying to check me out. Cute face, small waist, hazel brown eyes, caramel complected, smile like the sunrise. High cheek bones that remind you of Jeanette, body like Beyonce, the girls can't stand it."

I know I got skills on the mike...hahahahaha...sike. At a size 12, I embrace all my curves. And the guys don't seem to mind either. "Damn, she built like a stallion" is a phrase I have grown accustomed to over the years. Even my mother's friends noticed that I'm all grown up. "Damn Girl, you been eating your Wheaties."

Long, wet and wavy honey-blonde invisible braids is my hairstyle by choice. It's really convenient for a girl with such an active lifestyle. As for my daily makeup routine, it's none existent. All I need is my midnight black Maybelline Pulse mascara and my Bobbi Brown lip gloss.

People often ask me why I'm smiling every time they see me. That's me, showing all 32 teeth, trying to hold back my grin exposes my dimples. I have three piercings in each ear, but usually only wear one set of earrings. My nose ring looks more like a piece of glitter permanently stuck to my face. I used to have a belly ring but let it close up since my once flat stomach isn't so flat anymore. I have tattoos, but most of them are not visible while wearing clothes.

I have a pair of cherries on my right shoulder blade with the words 'Cherish Me' inscribed. Going across my lower back I have thirteen butterflies varying in sizes and colors with the words 'Fly Girl.' On the bottom of my left leg about three inches higher than my ankle, I have the words 'Brown Sugar'; A nick name given to me by a former boyfriend. And last (well at least for now) I have four hearts on my right foot.

I am a truly organized person. For starters, I think before I act. I don't know if one spontaneous bone exists in my whole body. I make daily to-do lists; for me they help me complete tasks quicker and more efficiently. I usually tackle the important things first. My favorite part is checking the job off the list. My calendar helps me manage my time wisely in order to keep up with appointments and meetings. The motto I live by is "If you are early, you're on time and if you are on time, you're late."

I absolutely hate clutter. My brother calls me a neat freak. But what's wrong with a color coordinated closet or an alphabetized DVD collection? I don't consider myself compulsive because I know when it's time to take a break. In a social situation I tend to introduce myself. Even if I am attracted to someone, I prefer to be the one pursued. I am not a coupon clipper; however I do shop for deals. I enjoy cooking and trying out new recipes, especially for someone I am dating. I almost never read a newspaper; the closest I come to a newspaper is picking up the Red Eye on my daily commute. I am not a morning person. I hate getting up early but I prefer to get my "To Do" list taken care of as soon as possible.

Everyone around me thinks I am the perfect size just as I am but I know I need to tone, tighten, and lose a few pounds (more like 15). I do not smoke and only have one or two drinks socially, which isn't often because I prefer a movie night any day over the club scene. If I have to go to a club, probably for a Ladies Night Out, then I like to hit a downtown spot. I like throwing social gatherings at home where Spades is the main attraction. I am very competitive so if you do not know the rules of the game, then now is not the time to show you.

I hate crossword puzzles and I suck at whistling. I need unlimited text messaging on my phone and can do without daytime minutes. I refuse to sit on a phone and listen to you breathe. I have been accused on more than one occasion of being a shopaholic. It's not like I buy on impulse, I will only buy something if it speaks to me. I wear a size 9 and a half in men's and 11 in women's shoes. I am lucky if I can find some cute shoes in my size so when I do, they instantly become a must have.

This entire chapter was kind of random. I just felt like sharing some little known facts about myself.

> *You can't lead the way, for yourself or others, if you don't truly know yourself, and that includes loving yourself unconditionally. This should be your first*

priority. When you know yourself, know what you stand for and what you want from life, you will be a happier and more productive person. Self-reflection is a great skill to learn. It not only teaches you how to pause and look at where you've been, but it allows you to understand others better.

Little brother gone astray

*M*y brother has a lot of tattoos, too. I think he became addicted though when he went to prison.

He went through processing (and for those unfamiliar with the term, processing includes taking an inventory of a new inmate's personal property, fingerprinting, photographs, personal searches, a change from street clothes to prison clothing, and an explanation of prison rules) with eleven tats, but 25 months later he has over sixty. According to my brother, "Lil Wayne ain't got shit on me."

Looking at his baby pictures you wouldn't think that one day this little boy would grow up to be a convicted felon, but just like so many other men in the African American community, he too has spent a fair share of time involved with the wrong side of the criminal justice system.

It all started back in high school, his sophomore year. He thought his football coach was showing favoritism and punishing him unfairly. In the middle of running laps he yelled out, "Fuck you, I quit." He went to the locker room and called me to pick him up.

"Why you leaving so early," I asked.

"I quit the team," he mumbled. And just like that he had gone from an honor roll student-athlete to cutting class and doing drugs with high school drop outs. He showed up to class high so often that the Dean made him enroll in a rehab program.

My mom knew he and his friends were smoking marijuana, and since her boyfriend (who by the way is another looser and to this day is sleeping on his mother's couch) refused to pay back the money she loaned him, she started stealing weed from him and giving it to my brother.

"Sell these for five dollars and sell these for ten," she explained. In her mind, it was a profitable idea; this way my brother could stop spending so much money with the 'weed man' and his friends could buy the drugs from him.

"France owed me money and since he wouldn't pay me back, I stole from his stash," she admitted.

My brother got a part time job working at Wendy's and the next thing I recall is him buying a new car. I knew he was doing something he didn't have any business doing because I didn't know too many 16-year-olds working at a fast food restaurant who could afford a two toned Monte Carlo sitting on 22 inch block rims with huge 12 inch kicker speakers in the trunk.

It wasn't long before I discovered that he had started selling drugs. Before long the neighborhood police knew him by his first name and it seemed like every other week I was getting a phone call informing me that my brother had another run in with the cops. It had become routine so I wasn't a bit surprised when my mom called me at 3 o'clock in the morning.

I was sleepy and a little pissed off because I had to get up early for class in the morning and the last thing I wanted to hear about was the drama going on with my brother. It didn't take me long to realize that this phone call was different from all the others.

"Hello," I grunted still laying face down on my pillow.

"Cierra, Courtney is in the hospital," my mom stammered. I flipped over in my twin bed and sat up staring at my white wall. Light barely came through the blinds on my window from the street lights on the side of my dorm.

"What, he's where?" I babbled.

"They beat him with a bat," she cried "He may have a concussion."

Later I learned that my brother and Greg, one of his jail bird friends, had gone to this party in the Englewood area. They were shooting dice; my brother had won a lot of money and was talking shit. The guys followed him out of the party and jumped him. Greg ran and left my brother there fighting 5 dudes by himself. He tried the best he could but he really didn't stand a chance. They beat him with a bat, took his money and his car keys, and left him in the middle of the street unconscious. They stole his radio out of his Monte Carlo and gave the keys back to Greg.

As soon as I heard what happened, I told my brother it was a set up. "You go to Greg's hood with him, you get beat up, he leave you, these are people he know, he brought you around these grimy niggas, he knew what was going down."

Seeing my brother like that made me want to go out and kill somebody. Knots all on his head, cuts covered his face. I could barely recognize him. I tried not to stare but his eyes were swollen shut. I hated seeing him like that. Revenge ran deep in my heart.

Somebody gotta pay for this, I thought. When he got out of the hospital he stayed in the crib and my mom nursed his wounds.

After he graduated high school, my brother needed a change of scenery, so he left to go to California. He planned to stay with our big cousin, Bo, and his baby mama, and he had convinced my mother that Bo was a good influence on him.

Two days before he was scheduled to return to Chicago he got locked up on a million dollar bond. Turns out my brother, my big cousin, his homey, and this white chick tried to rob the drug connect. Their timing was perfect; the big time drug dealer had left his sister home alone. It was now or never.

Courtney was the get-away driver so he stayed in the Hummer truck. The white girl pretended that her car had broken down to try to get access into the drug house. Bo and his friend were waiting off to the side planning on bum rushing the door. They jumped out with their guns locked and loaded but were unaware that the sister's boyfriend was also in the house. He grabbed her inside and slammed the front door. They ran back to the car, but instead of leaving, they just sat there.

"They not gone call the police, this is a damn drug house," Bo assumed.

Well, needless to say, they did call the police. Everyone was arrested, including the drug house residents, and my brother stayed in custody well over nine months while he fought the case. The public defender urged him to accept the plea bargain in return for a lighter sentence, but considering it was his first offense, he thought the judge would take that into consideration. He thought wrong because both Courtney and Bo were found guilty. My brother was sentenced to four years, but would only end up doing a little over two. He walked out the court room handcuffed with his head hanging down. My mother stood up and said, "Hold your head up, I'm still proud of you. You're still my son, so hold your head up high.

> *No one is perfect. Through failures and mistakes you really learn life's lessons. Being perfect doesn't teach us how to cope but tragedy does. Just make sure the mistakes you make are your own decisions and take responsibility for them. Don't get caught up in someone else's mess.*

Institutionalized

While waiting to be transferred to state prison, my brother quickly discovered "if u can make it thru the county jail. U can make it thru prison." My mother and I were worried sick about him. We couldn't visit often due to the distance, our phone bill was sky high and we were struggling financially to keep money on his books. Although he was homesick, he says it was better that he wasn't from California.

"Why you say it's better that you from Chicago?" I asked him in a letter.

"These niggas really gang bang in LA. It's a way of life for them," he responded.

My brother adjusted to the prison environment rather quickly. He didn't keep to himself but he only interacted with other inmates to a certain extent. "If u didn't do what I did, it was no point for us to kick it. You got some dudes that's passing needles doing heroine, I don't want to mess with them. They in serious debt with niggas on the yard. Then you got Muslims who always asking for a veggie tray but gone eat a pork chop sandwich and get a white woman as soon as they get out."

Survival seemed to be the key denominator, so my brother used his food service job as a commodity to obtain personal items he wouldn't otherwise be able to receive.

"That's how I got all my tattoos. I use to steal fruit from the kitchen so they could make wine called white lightening. I had three people cooking for me: Manson, Night Owl and Fred, they were all lifers. Night Owl made it the best so he would sell out real quick. Crack, my tattoo artist was this skinny half-pint looking nigga. He was a straight alcoholic. All he wanted to do was get drunk, get high, and do tattoos."

He also fell into a pattern to help pass his time. Everyday his program was the same. 4am, working in the kitchen pushing trays. 9:15am, yard time where he and his celly got in shape. Sometimes other prisoners would join in, but most didn't last. While telling me about his workout he bragged, "The train don't stop. Passengers hop on and off, but we were driving that motherfucker."

At 11am the guards performed a count of the inmate population. According to Courtney "they gone count their money four or five times a day. That's their cash." Around 11:15am he played dominoes with Redbone, an old guy serving life who received disability checks on his books. Finally about 1pm he showered, read a couple chapters in his current book, wrote a letter and took a nap.

One time, my mother and I went to visit my brother and I noticed some changes in his behavior. For instance, he was constantly darting his eyes back and fourth, surveying the room.

"Are you paying attention to me" I asked.

"Girl, I hear everything you saying."

"Well, why aren't you looking at me when I talk to you?"

He explained how he had to be aware of his surroundings at all times. The prison was racially segregated. Any minor incident could cause a riot. He told us that the week before, this young Mexican got into it with this old white man. He tried to rush him off the toilet.

"Hurry up old man, I gotta boo boo." The old man ignored him and took his sweet time taking his shit. When he finally got done, the Mexican pushed the old man out of the way.

"Fuck you," shouted the old man. The Mexican responded by punching him in the face. And just like that a riot broke out. I was shocked at the trivial events that could spark such a disturbance, but my brother quickly taught me an unwritten rule of prison.

"You not supposed to touch another race. You not supposed to share food with another race. In here, you stick with your own kind."

My brother went on with his lesson explaining the prison alliance.

"The Blacks, Chinese, and Indians are allies, but its crazy cuz the Chinese mess with the White boys, but the Chinese don't mess with the Mexicans, White boys mess with these dudes but they don't mess with us. So it's kinda like we not allies anyway."

My brother did his time and didn't allow his time to "whoop him". Instead he made the best of his situation. Since his release, one of the factors that motivate him to stay on the right path is witnessing repeat offenders recycled in and out of prison.

"They like it better in than out." He personally dislikes the label 'institutionalized' because to him an institutionalized individual is that person who prefers the prison environment over society. These guys' fathers served time in prison, so did their brothers and uncles. He probably was conceived on a conjugal visit. They have nothing or no one to go home to. This prison life is all they know.

He also prefers the term inmate over the labels convict, jailbird or prisoner because "After you get out of prison, you can drop the term inmate, but the convict and felony labels stick with you forever."

On his last night in prison his homeboy made some gumbo and he ate his last prison meal. He took a shower and received his last prison hair cut. He gave away all his belongings which included shoes, a boom box radio and some clothes. He was glad to rid himself of the prison reminders. He didn't even go to sleep his last night. He smiled from ear to ear as he lay on his bunk.

" *Everyone learns about life in their own way. I had a traditional college education and my lessons came through the trials that go with that. My brother's education came from the streets, but his lessons are just as valid and as valuable to him as mine are to me.*

He learned the hard way that the streets don't love you, and family will always be by his side.

Do as I say, not as I do

I love my momma to death. She raised me and my brother by herself and I never once remember her complaining. She's an attractive, intelligent, independent woman, but when it comes to men she doesn't always make the best decisions. Although she was the youngest of ten, she was the first college graduate from her family. She seemed to be on the right path, so how did this southern belle end up with a Chicago hustler and why did she stay with him after he began abusing her?

I wonder if my overprotective grandmother is to blame for her lack of first-hand experience. She had to learn about the birds and the bees from her college roommates and she promised herself that she would have a more open relationship with her own children. People are shocked when they learn that my mother was the first person I confided in when I was thinking about having sex. She taught me to stand up for myself.

"Girl, if you don't get out there and defend yourself I will beat your butt myself," she'd say. She also taught me the value of keeping a home in order. "I don't need a dishwasher, that's what I got you and your brother for," she joked.

Her sheltered upbringing included a strict Baptist home where she woke up at the crack of dawn to pick cotton and was forced to attend church three times a week. Growing up, my mom had a wonderful connection with her father. She remembers him as "The Sunday School teacher who sang songs in church that made the women cry, and the man who took care of his family."

Her relationship with her mom was at the opposite end of the spectrum. My grandmother, Naomi, was afraid her baby girl would get pregnant while she was away at school. My mother didn't get knocked up, but she did get knocked around. In her junior year of college she met a guy named

Joseph Harris. Everybody called him Lil Joe; he was from East Saint Louis. Eventually they moved off campus together in a trailer park not far from her school. Since she was no longer staying on campus, she started receiving food stamps.

One day, some money came up missing so she confronted Lil Joe about it. The accusation really pissed him off so he jumped on her. When her college roommates, Darinette and Terri, came to visit; they immediately noticed her black eye. My mom confessed what happened and Darinette did not hesitate to call my mother's brother. Once Uncle Larry found out, him and his brothers came to pay Lil Joe a visit. I asked her if the relationship ended after the incident, and she responded, "They beat him up real bad, so bad that he stopped beating me. He knew they would come back. He knew I had five brothers...but we stayed together."

But why did she have such low expectations for herself and why did she put up with so much bullshit from men?

Growing up, my biggest fear was making the same mistakes she had when it came to relationships. I vowed to myself that I wouldn't make the same bad choices. I recall an argument we had. She didn't approve of this guy I was dating, but according to me, it wasn't none of her damn business.

I yelled at the top of my lungs, "How can you out of all people try to give me advice about men?" I still remember the look in her eyes. I stumbled over my words as I tried to explain.

"I'm... I'm sorry mom, I... I didn't mean it. I...I was just upset." She didn't respond. She walked away teary eyed and closed her bedroom door behind her. The truth of the matter is, I did mean it, I meant every word. I just didn't mean to say it out loud.

Sometimes I used to wonder if my dating decisions would have been any better if my father was still alive. Then I quickly realized that they probably would have been worse. My dad was a hustler and he beat the shit out of my mom. Fuck it! Even I can do better than an abusive drug dealer.

> *I didn't realize it then, but my mother was actually trying to prevent me from making some of the same mistakes she had made when it came to re-*

lationships with men. I vowed to never make those same mistakes, but I failed horribly. I have dated player, jocks, manipulators, abusers (physical and mental), somebody's baby daddy, and a married man.

For some reason I keep making bad decisions in this area, and I often find myself in a situation-ship dealing with a man who is emotionally unavailable. I guess I'm trying to protect myself from hurt and pain, and I'm working to recognize and correct this. I'm trying to make better choices when it comes to men, and to confront or leave a bad relationship before I sleep with a man so I can have a happier healthier future.

Sucker for love

Why does this always happen to me? I meet a guy, I'm feeling him and I think he's feeling me. He tells me what I want to hear and I actually believe his lying ass. I think he's the love of my life, possibly my future husband. But sooner, rather than later, the relationship ends. Either I get bored or the guy loses interest. I'm left feeling unsatisfied and even worse for adding to my number. You know, the number of people we have had sexual intercourse with. Now I KNOW YOU ARE DYING TO KNOW, BUT I AM NOT GOING TO REVEAL THAT NUMBER TO YOU. Sometimes I wish I had a reset button so I could start all over from scratch. I know a 'reset' button doesn't exist but you can't fault a girl for dreaming.

One day I came to the conclusion that I would be celibate. Yeah, that's right, I was gonna try that shit them monks in the monasteries do. I decided to make the change for a variety of reasons. To begin, I was tired of being treated like a rag doll by the opposite sex. I wanted more out of a relationship than just the physical aspect. I wanted to only share myself with someone who would appreciate and cherish me. Can you believe I went a whole nine months without getting any?

It wasn't like I was missing much. Half of the time he's the only one who's satisfied. That might be too much information but it's the truth. Either the guy is a two-minute-man or just so small that I can't feel a thing. Are you kidding me? You got the nerves to wear a magnum? Have you ever seen a baggy condom? The shit is hilarious. I'm sitting there thinking, Nigger you know you can't fit no magnum. Are you trying to make yourself feel better or something?

And even worse than the dude with the baggy condom is the guy who tries to go down and doesn't have the slightest idea of what he's doing down there. I appreciate the effort honey, but please don't give me special attention if you don't have skills with your tongue. I use to hate getting head. It was totally disgusting until I found a guy who knew how to please me. The brother was really taking care of his business. He had me crawling up walls and trying to run from him. I never knew it could feel like that. He went for hours and hours. I still remember it like it was just yesterday.

I was feeling a bit depressed. My boyfriend and I had gotten into yet another argument and I was tired and drained. My friend called right on time because I really needed him. Now, I am not accustomed to going outside my relationship seeking advice, but tonight I just needed the male's perspective. My friend of four years and I talked for over an hour when a knock came at the door.

"Hold on a sec, someone's at door." My unexpected guest turned out to be my friend whom I was speaking with over the phone. I was so excited to see him; he always made me feel better. Once upon a time, he expressed his interest in me. He wanted to be more than just friends, but I didn't want to ruin our friendship. Deep down inside, I've always been attracted to him. Who wouldn't though, he is tall, dark and handsome. He is a frequent visitor to the gym, too. He keeps his body tight. I can see his muscles popping out from underneath his white V-neck shirt. His pearly white smile looks great against his chocolate skin. And his braids are always neat.

We continued our conversation about my relationship issues. He could tell I was stressed so he offered to give me a shoulder massage which eventually turned into a full body rub down. He lit a candle, busted out the baby oil and had Raheem Devaughn playing in the background.

Raheem's 'Desire' lyrics coupled with the strong yet gentle touch of this man relaxed me tremendously. I knew this was wrong but it felt so damn good. He touched me like I had never been touched before. He knew what the art of seduction required. He was patient and he understood my psyche.

First, he undressed me with his eyes; I helped by un-buttoning my blouse, unsnapping my bra and lying on my stomach on top of my bed. After the full hour massage, which by the way was better than the professionals, he turned me on my back and ran his fingers across my body then between my legs. He kissed me all over. He spelled his name with his tongue on my stomach. He knew what he was doing and I enjoyed being teased. The anticipation was half the fun and when I couldn't take it any longer he slid his tongue below my naval taking it nice and slow and then he licked me between my thighs.

I wanted him to continue but needed him to stop. He was quite experienced; I didn't know it was supposed to feel like this. He licked, and kissed, and sucked, and fingered me. This level of special attention could whip a girl. I ran my finger through his braids and squeezed my legs tight around his head. I pushed myself further up the bed, trying to escape, it was feeling too good, and when I couldn't take it any longer I exploded.

He whispered in my ear, "Damn, baby, you taste good " He inserted his manhood into my V-jay-jay and made her purr like a small kitten.

"Oooo, baby, I like that. Right there, don't stop. You're so deep I can feel you in my stomach," I whispered.

He told me how good it felt being inside me. He didn't have to tell me though; I knew I had that good-good. He wanted to make me feel better and he definitely accomplished that.

After we made love, he kissed me softly on my forehead. We lay there side by side, shocked and amazed at what had just occurred. So many pent up desires had finally been released. I walked him to the front door and hugged him goodbye.

"Thanks for stopping by, I really enjoyed your company," I grinned.

He kissed me on my cheek and asked, "Now what, Cierra?"

"What do you mean?" I responded as if I didn't know what he really meant. He wanted to know what would happen next between us? He wanted to know if our night of passion had changed our friendship and if so, in what way? He wanted to know if I would break up with my boyfriend? His "Now what?" encompassed a lot of questions. Questions I just wasn't prepared to answer at that point.

"" *Many women (and men) are in love with the idea of love. They just want someone in their lives and often go blindly into a relationship ignoring all the warning signs. Safe sex protects your future. Use a condom. Enough said!*

No place like home

*L*ooking for a home can be time consuming. There are a lot of factors involved in one's decision to purchase a home. Shopping around for homes with my mom brought up some old memories.

While riding in the car, listening to Tom Joyner's morning show and singing along with Mary J. Blidge's "I'm Not Going To Cry", my mom and I talked about our good times in South Holland. And now eight years later, we are back out house hunting.

Once again we encountered the same problem with the deal falling through. It felt good that we were finally moving out of our "temporary apartment" and into a 2-flat apartment with a full basement in the city. This 5 bedroom, 3 bath Bronzeville beauty had been recently remodeled and included granite countertops, cathedral ceilings, hardwood floors, two fireplaces and a huge master suite. Despite the unfinished basement, it was listed way under market value, so my mom jumped on the quick sale.

Three months later, the basement is finally complete with 2 bedrooms and 2 full baths, hardwood floors and granite countertops and is now my condo. And my favorite part of my condo is the walk in closet and 6 foot Jacuzzi tub where I enjoy candle lit bubble baths. We plan on living here for years and years to come. I am glad we are finally settled.

While my brother was incarcerated, the bills got a little bit more than my mother could bear. She didn't have a choice but to move on campus with me in my apartment. She lived rent free for damn near four months without anyone noticing. She was able to stack her money and pay off some debt.

After I graduated, we end up getting evicted out of our temporary apartment. It wasn't like we couldn't afford the rent, but my mom refused to sign another yearly lease because in less than a month, or so we thought at the time, we would be moving into our Bronzeville 2-flat. The landlord kicked us out and my mother's friend was kind enough to let us stay in his studio apartment, which he was using for storage space.

It was so tiny and dirty, but we made it work. We cleaned up the space and moved most of our belongings to Public Storage. Closing the deal on the 2-flat took longer than anticipated, and Jimmy wasn't expecting for us to be staying as long as we did so he decided to go up on the rent, which me or my mother couldn't understand because we didn't even have a working bathroom. We bathed in the kitchen sink.

Once again, we didn't have anyplace to go. We were literally homeless when Jimmy kicked us out. We debated about going to stay at a hotel, and I was depressed that it had come to this. All of our bags were packed and we were on our way to check into the hotel when my ex boyfriend called and said me and my mother could move in with him. We paid rent and helped out with the groceries. I wasn't working at the time so I made sure to do my part by cooking and keeping the house spotless.

I appreciate Kevin for allowing us to crash at his place,

but I have to admit that the living arrangements were kind of uncomfortable. He told me he had moved on with his life, but having me around brought up old feelings he didn't know were still there. I didn't want to mess up his life; he seemed to be doing well for himself. He was working and going to school full time. It was bitter-sweet for him once we finally moved into our new home in Bronzeville. He had gotten accustomed to having me around and just like that I was gone again from his life. Not permanently because we still talked on the phone, but he couldn't walk through his front door and see me anymore. I had moved on.

> *I found myself homeless with no where to go, so I told myself every night, "The best is yet to come." Things will go wrong, sometimes hopelessly wrong. When you find yourself in a situation where it seems like there is nothing left, remember that this is not the end and things always have a way of turning around.*

Smokey

*O*n November 2009, I was hired by the U.S. Census Bureau as a temporary office clerk. Although the position is short term, it offers great pay which I definitely need while I am in between jobs. I basically handle administrative tasks like answering phones, filing documents and inputting data into the computer. Only thirty more minutes before I get off, I thought. Damn, why did I just look up at that clock? I have officially stopped time. This thirty minutes is probably gonna feel more like two hours.

"Cierra, Jasmine just texted me... You want to go out tonight? " asked Tiffany, my coworker.

"To be honest, I really don't feel like clubbing, but I guess I can take one for the team. Where y'all trying to go?" I asked.

"Jaz was thinking Ontourage or Vain. I never have been to Vain before."

"Well it doesn't matter to me, I know promoters at both spots so I can get us on the list."

By the time I glanced back at the clock it was only ten minutes left. I felt the vibration from my phone on my hip. This is the second time my mom has called, I thought. I hope she was able to get the TV today from the Black Friday sale at Walmart. I will just call her when I get off; only eight minutes and counting.

The U.S. Census Bureau was probably the only government agency open the day after Thanksgiving. By 4:55 p.m. everyone in the office had already cleared their desks, packed their bags and put on their coats. I was bundled up pretty tight with my black scarf and gloves and my gray wool coat fastened with its fashion belt. From my shoulder hung my black leather Kenneth Cole briefcase. My hair was pulled back with a black headband. I power walked to my car holding an empty Tupperware lunch container in one hand and my car keys in the other. I started my engine and called my mom back. She picked up on the first ring.

"Yeah, Morn, what's up?"

Between her sobs I heard her say "Cierra, the dog next door killed Smokey."

Tears immediately formed. "What! Did you have him on the leash?"

"Yes, Cierra, I got to go, I'm talking to the police."

I could barely see the road. I cried uncontrollably. There were times when I looked down and my speed read 95 mph. I shook my head and beat the steering wheel with my fists.

"Ok Cierra, calm down" I told myself. "Just make it home safe." I was driving too fast, I knew I should slow down, but I had to travel 25 miles before I made it home. I slowed down a little, now I was only doing 80mph in a 55 speed limit zone. I zoomed down I-57, weaving in and out of traffic and made it home in less than 20 minutes. I pulled onto my block and two police cars and an animal control van was parked outside my home. I threw the gear in park and sprinted inside. I had never run so fast in heels before. Click, click, clat was the sound I made hustling up the front porch steps. I busted through the front door to find strange faces standing in my living room.

My mom was talking to a police officer and my brother was sitting on the couch when I asked, "What happened? Where's Smokey?"

The man in the brown uniform answered, "He's outside on the neighbor's property."

"What, y'all left him out there?" I yelled. I walked toward the door but the police in his Chicago Blue uniform stood in front of me.

"I don't think you should go out there."

"Cierra, you can't move him now," said my mother. I sat on the couch and continued to sob. My mascara, eye shadow and eyeliner were smudged.

"SMOKEY, NO NO NO," I cried out. I screamed shaking my head. "Why did this have to happen? How did this happen?" The last question was directed to my mom. She was the one who had Smokey when the vicious pit bull next door snatched him through the gate. She was the one always leaving him outside by himself. She was the one who claimed that the pit bull would only run up and down the gate with Smokey.

It didn't really cross my mind at the time, but later I thought about how hurt my mom must have been. Technically, Smokey was her dog. He was a gift given to her by her ex. My mother and Smokey had become really close. He kept her company while I was away at school and my brother was locked up. He would sit on her lap and sleep on the floor at the foot of her bed. He was such a lovable dog. Watching him being attacked by the pit bull must have been even more devastating.

"I told you he was dangerous," I cried. Not even three weeks prior the brown 85lb pit bull had bitten my mother's friend, Chris. He had lost so much blood. The blood dripped everywhere as he rushed to the bathroom sink. His middle finger on his right hand was ripped open. His cousin took him to Providence Hospital up the street. What started out as a fun-filled day with family, friends and football, ended up with a man in the hospital. The Bears lost the game against the Cardinals, but unfortunately, the pit bull next door that the owners claimed "doesn't bite" had just bite someone.

"What's going to happen to the other dog? Is he going to be put to sleep?" The long winded answers given by the animal control officer seemed to mean NO.

I walked outside still crying my eyes out and there he was "the number one man in my life, my baby, my Smoke dog" laying there lifeless. My brother and the policeman covered him with a towel and placed him in a Sam's Club grocery bag. I didn't even notice my mom walk up.

"No, Cierra, don't look at him," she warned as I gently opened the bag. I felt his fur. He looked as if he was sleeping.

"Only seven years old and it ended like this" I cried. "WHY, WHY?" I pleaded.

After the police left, my bother carried the Sam's Club bag and a shovel across the street to an open field. Mom and I followed and I watched him as he dug deeper and deeper into the dirt. I was afraid when he lifted the towel from the Sam's Club bag and placed Smokey in the ground. They told me that the pit bull damn near ripped his neck off. They didn't want me to see the evidence so my brother kept Smokey wrapped up in a burgundy bath towel as he placed him in the grave. I stood there frozen as my mother and brother covered my dog with dirt. I couldn't believe my eyes. I could accept it if he passed away from old age, but this, this was just brutal murder. Smokey was killed and there wasn't anything anyone could do to bring him back.

"Don't cry, Cierra," my brother said as he ushered me away from the grave site. "I will get you another puppy."

"I don't want another one. No dog can replace him," I sobbed. I knew my brother had good intentions. He was just trying to make me feel better. Despite all the chaos around us, he kept a level head. I could really tell how much he had changed since his time in California State Penitentiary.

I realized that my brother went in a boy but came out a man. He had done a lot of growing up in prison. This was probably the best thing that could have happened to him. A blessing in disguise, I thought.

When the three of us walked back to our house, my mother's friend, Milliscent, stood on the porch. She hugged my mom and then me. "Baby I knew you would take it the hardest. I know how much you loved Smokey. I told my family to pray for y 'all."

I embraced Milliscent and cried over her shoulder. I just wanted to wake up from this bad dream. We went inside and I sat on the couch Milliscent put one hand on my back and the other on my head. "Dear Lord, we ask you today," she began to pray. "In your son Jesus name, Amen," she concluded.

I wanted them to pay. "What can we do?" I asked out loud to anyone who was listening. My brother wanted to poison the dog.

"Now Courtney, you remember what happened to Vick. You can go to jail for that," warned Milliscent. I guess my brother realized what he had been saying.

"Awwww, naw, I can't go back to prison. I ain't never going back there." My mom was thinking about the legal aspect.

"We go to court in two weeks," I replied. "I have friends who have been afraid to walk down my walk-way because the dog can fit his head through the gate. I could get them to sign a statement about how dangerous the dog is."

"Now you thinking, Baby Girl," my mother replied. Milliscent began writing the statement; she is an English major so I trusted her with that responsibility.

"Next you need to take pictures of the gate and get some measurements" said Milliscent. You can show them in court and give the judge a better idea of the scene of the crime. We were strategizing our case when the doorbell rung. The next door neighbor and owner of the killer dog stood in the doorway. My mother invited him in.

"I'm sorry for your loss. I'm sorry this happened," he apologized. My mom spoke briefly with him.

How many times have I warned them about that damn dog? "No he doesn't bite" they claimed. "He barks to protect the property," they said. I knew that was a bunch of bullshit. The fucking dog has teeth.

"What do you mean he doesn't bite? All fucking dogs bite." I couldn't even bring myself to look up at him. I wanted him to feel my pain. I wanted him to lose his dog, too.

A little while after he left, I grabbed my coat and headed to my basement apartment. I walked in and my brother shouted, "TaaDaaaa." I glanced over at the 50 inch flat screen TV.

"Mommie already told me that y'all picked it up from Walmart." I walked to my bedroom, lit a candle, kicked off my heels, and took off my dress pants and sweater. I kept on my black socks and put on some black sweat pants and a black long sleeved thermal. I lay in the dark underneath my brown and beige suede cover. I cried until I couldn't cry anymore. I walked in my bathroom to wipe my face. My eyes were swollen and bloodshot red. Next, I rustled through old photo albums and gathered pictures of

Smokey. I posted a status on my Facebook page in memory of him. My friends were concerned.

"Sorry for your loss". "R.I.P. Smokey". "I can't imagine how you feel, my dog is like a part of my fam, too". "OMG". "I can't believe this happened". "Gone but never forgotten".

People texted and called my phone all night. One person, the only person I have ever really loved, offered to stop by and check on me. Fifteen minutes later, Kevin stood at my door. I let him in and we walked to my bedroom.

"You were lying in the dark?" he asked.

"Yeah," was the only word I could muster myself to say.

He updated me about the things that were going on in his life. His nephew was in town for the holiday. He really liked his new Radio/IV class. He was slacking off at work because of school and his father didn't like that too much. He put a smile on my face and for the first time all night, I was laughing. My ex boyfriend of 2 and a half years had always been there when I needed him the most. During my collegiate career as a student/athlete. When my coach was tripping and making me ride the bench. When I was having roommate issues. When I tore my ACL he helped nurse me back to health. Through the tough tests he helped me study for. When my little brother went to prison and now when my dog, Smokey, was killed.

I laughed to keep from crying, but that only lasted for so long before I couldn't contain myself any longer. He held me in his arms, he rubbed me on my back, he kissed me on my forehead and said, "Everything gonna be alright."

It was at this very moment that I realized how much I appreciated Kevin for being a true friend. He always came to my aid when I was experiencing tough times. He had to get up early for class in the morning but he held me until I fell asleep. When he got ready to leave, he whispered, "I will let myself out."

After he left, I cried some more. But these tears were not as sad. I reminisced as I flipped through some of Smokey's photos and cried myself to sleep.

> *There will be times in life when you'll cry for the loss of a loved one. Don't stop the tears from coming. They're a healing mechanism that will relieve some of the pain and sorrow you're feeling, making way for tomorrow's love and happiness.*

My life

My life if good and I still have a lot to work on, but that's was life is - a work in progress. I'm still searching for my career, among other things.

Oh, and I almost forgot, yours truly was featured in the February 2010 edition of Black Hair Magazine! I'm so excited; I don't even know what to do with myself It's not like I won an Oscar or discovered the cure for AIDS or anything, but I feel very lucky to be recognized by a magazine that I love and respect so much. Especially in their issue featuring First Lady Michelle Obama on the cover (Barack is a lucky guy).

To see my name and pictures in Black Hair is beyond incredible. It's kind of a big deal to have landed on the pages of a national magazine! I even started dating this terrific guy. We have so many shared interests and he treats me like a queen. I have a good feeling about this one, but let's not get ahead of ourselves.

Last but not least, I visited my father's grave site. It's located in Burr Oak Cemetery near Alsip. When I heard that four people had been accused of reselling plots and dumping the remains of old bodies in an empty, abandoned lot, I was overcome with emotion. After searching the cemetery, I finally located my father's grave. The grave marker is all that is left to mark his exact location.

This is the third time I have stood on this the bumpy terrain. The first time I was two years old. I barely remember coming here, but I have an old obituary for proof. The second time I visited with my half sister, Shaunta, and my younger brother Courtney. I recall placing flowers on his grave and shedding a few tears. But this time, I went alone. I was able to pray in front of it and talk to him. Tell him about my life, the one he never got to witness.

My family photos

*My mom and dad
on their wedding day*

*Me and my father,
William (Billy). I had just
turned one. This is one
of the few photos
I have of us together*

*My brother and me
hugging it out*

My grandfather
and his sister, Lena.
Rest in peace my angels

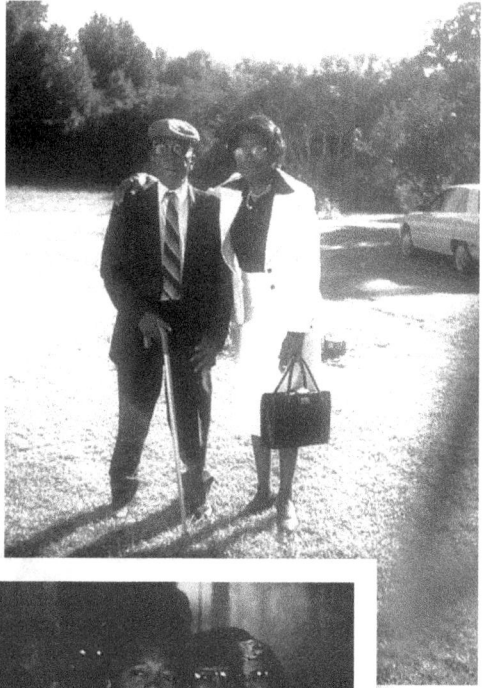

Grandma and Paw Paw
sitting on the
first pew at church

Grandma and me

My dad in his red leather suit. You couldn't tell him nothing that day

Dad at the bar with his cowboy hat

My mom and her boyfriend, Johnny. Besides my grandfather, the only real father figure I've really known

Graduating
with my Master's Degree
with my support system

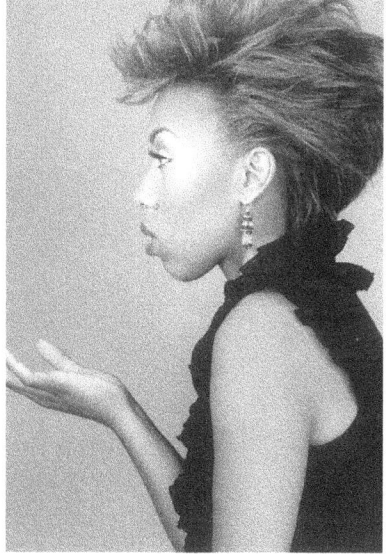

One of many
of my modeling
photos.
This one was
in a magazine!

Photoshoot, boy i use to love my micro briads

My dad and me.
I miss you more than
you know.
We will meet again
'after while'
and maybe
I can finally be
Daddy's Little Girl

Copyright © 2015 by Cierra Thurman
Written Ambition Publishing
P.O. Box 53297
Chicago, IL 60653

Edited by Lee Caleca
Cover Design and Layout by Zgola Alexey

Printed by CreateSpace, An Amazon.com Company

www.ingramcontent.com/pod-product-compliance
Lightning Source LLC
Chambersburg PA
CBHW051831090426
42736CB00011B/1753